Nightmares

NIGHTMARES

THE DARK SIDE OF DREAMS AND DREAMING

STASE MICHAELS

Author of *A Little Bit of Dreams*

STERLING ETHOS

New York

This book is dedicated to those in pain and to healers—
as professionals in many walks of life or healers of
the heart—who seek to alleviate others' pain.

STERLING ETHOS
New York

An Imprint of Sterling Publishing Co., Inc.
1166 Avenue of the Americas
New York, NY 10036

STERLING ETHOS and the distinctive Sterling Ethos logo
are registered trademarks of Sterling Publishing Co., Inc.

ISBN 978-1-4549-2737-2

Distributed in Canada by Sterling Publishing Co., Inc.
c/o Canadian Manda Group, 664 Annette Street Toronto, Ontario M6S 2C8, Canada
Distributed in the United Kingdom by GMC Distribution Services
Castle Place, 166 High Street, Lewes, East Sussex BN7 1XU, England
Distributed in Australia by NewSouth Books
University of New South Wales, Sydney, NSW 2052, Australia

For information about custom editions, special sales, and premium and corporate purchases,
please contact Sterling Special Sales at 800-805-5489 or specialsales@sterlingpublishing.com.

Manufactured in Malaysia

4 6 8 10 9 7 5 3

Cover design by Igor Satanovsky
Interior design by Christine Heun

sterlingpublishing.com

For image credits, see page 202

Contents

CHAPTER ONE
Welcome to the World of Nightmares, 1

CHAPTER TWO
Analyze a Dream in Minutes, 11

CHAPTER THREE
Nightmares That Digest Fears and Anxieties, 33

CHAPTER FOUR
Nightmares That Confront You about You!, 41

CHAPTER FIVE
Nightmares as True, Literal Warnings, 77

CHAPTER SIX
Recurring Nightmares, 103

CHAPTER SEVEN
Death in Dreams, 123

CHAPTER EIGHT
Super-Intense Nightmares, 155

CHAPTER NINE
Common Nightmare Symbols, 183

FINAL THOUGHTS
The Author's Last Words on Nightmares, 194

INDEX, 196
ABOUT THE AUTHOR, 202
IMAGE CREDITS, 202

CHAPTER ONE

Welcome to the World of Nightmares

When you get a text message or phone call from someone you love, you trust the source and instantly pick up. A nightmare has a bad rap as a frightening message that many run from. Not so! Even when a communication is scary, ditch preconceptions and welcome a nightmare as a conversation you want to have with a best friend—the wiser part of you.

JUST FOR FUN, TAKE THIS NIGHTMARE QUIZ:

Which of these statements about nightmares is true?

A. When you dream about someone who died, it can be an actual visit.

B. A nightmare about a disaster can be a true warning.

C. Nightmares have a hidden, yet constructive, message.

D. All of the above.

As the following chapters explain, the answer is (D): all of the above statements can be true. Dreams about the dead are often actual visits from a loved one who has passed on. In terms of warnings, dreams have warned many about an upcoming disaster or challenge. And like all dreams, a nightmare can bring help—if you unravel the map that points to the treasured message. *Hint:* Getting the message is easy. Chapter Three outlines a fast and easy way to find the meaning of a dream, including nightmares, with more hints scattered throughout the book.

Which of these statements about nightmares is false?

A. If you feel terrified and see yourself falling in a dream, you can die.

B. If you dream about a coffin, it means that someone will die.

C. If someone sleepwalks during a nightmare, they can harm someone.

D. All of the above.

The answer is a resounding (D): all of the above statements are false. The old wives' tale that you can die if you dream that you are falling is a crock. There is no such thing as a symbol that "always" means the same thing for everyone: falling is a metaphor for losing control or feeling as if life is not on firm ground;

like all symbols, it has a different meaning for different dreamers. This basic fact about symbols also rules out the misconception that dreams about a coffin are a sign that someone will die.

On to the sleepwalking statement. Research shows that while you dream, the large muscles of your body that control the arms and legs are paralyzed. The part of the brain that controls gross movements is on hold as you dream, so you cannot sleepwalk during a nightmare. Brain wave patterns during sleep show that you dream during Stage 1 of normal sleep, the level that is closest to being awake, so you dream when you are almost awake! Sleepwalking, on the other hand, happens during a deep sleep stage. A sleepwalker can experience random images, even scary ones, but a sleepwalker is not experiencing a full dream or nightmare. That is why, even during a blood-curdling nightmare, the potential to harm someone is extremely low, or negligible.

UNDERSTANDING NIGHTMARES

Understanding a nightmare is like attending the best Halloween costume party ever. When you arrive, your favorite TV and movie stars are waiting to greet you. All the guests race through a terrifying haunted house complete with fog, ghosts, ghouls, and gore. Fueled by adrenaline, you end up on a dimly lit dance floor, screaming—yet entertained. As you catch your breath, you realize that everything you just experienced was an entertaining façade that also boggled your mind. Even though it was scary, it made you let loose, transform, and experience the moment in a new way. Comparing nightmares to a Halloween party may sound crazy, yet it parallels what is true. Most of the time, a nightmare is a regular dream dressed up in a scary costume. Of course, there are exceptions. There are always exceptions. More on that later.

Dreams Versus Nightmares

How does a nightmare differ from a dream? A nightmare is different—yet the same. Dreams and nightmares both bring a message that can steer you past a challenge, provide insights about people, and give hints about how to resolve a problem. The main difference is that a nightmare is scary.

So the real question becomes: *Why* does a dream turn into a nightmare, and how does it happen? The quick answer describes a domino effect that goes like this: Anxiety makes you afraid. You fear the unknown, you resist what you fear, and you back away from what you do not want to confront. Fear distorts what you see and feel, including dream images. Suppose you see a dog walking down a dark street at midnight; as it approaches, dark shadows make it look terrifying, even if the pooch is friendly. Fear distorts a dream message, forcing dream characters and objects to hide behind scary costumes.

A nightmare also differs from a dream in power and energy. Emotionally, a dream can feel like a gentle rain or downpour; a nightmare lashes out with the power of a thunderstorm or hurricane that will not be ignored. A dream is a polite invitation. A nightmare pounds at your door, screaming, until you answer.

Where Do Nightmares Come From?

Like most dreams, nightmares are messages from your wiser, inner self, as a shout about something urgent that needs your attention. For believers, on a rare occasion a nightmare can be a heads-up from a guardian angel or a warning from the Divine itself. Joseph received a dream advising him to leave Bethlehem and flee to Egypt with Mary and Jesus, to avoid Herod's sword. Joseph's dream happened centuries ago as a notable event in Christian history, yet many still experience dream warnings. For those who are curious about how a dream happens, later sections provide a glimpse into the mechanics of a dream.

Scares Can Be Good for You

Most nightmares target a dreamer's anxieties, as a helping hand from the psyche. Sometimes the helping hand arrives as a nightmare. Why? Like a kick in the pants, sometimes a good scare can trigger a positive reaction. A man dreams that everyone except him gets promoted. The dream terrifies him, yet it also spurs him to get off his butt and take courses to improve his career skills. A scary dream can mirror a clash in a relationship, like the woman who dreams that a dog bites her hand. Her dream parallels a boyfriend's verbal put-downs: when she draws a line in the sand and tells him to back off, the nightmares disappear. A senior approaching retirement has nightmares about being stranded on a boat in the middle the ocean, as a fear of not being able to cope on a retirement income. It motivates him to make a new financial plan, for added security. Yes, terrifying dreams throw you into a maze of uncertainty. But they also include a message that shows the way out; and if you look closely, you can find that arrow.

Nightmares as Serious Red Flags

Most nightmares deal with day-to-day activities; however, if you have an emotional skeleton in your closet, a nightmare can point out a hidden, serious issue. Lynda was a divorced woman in her thirties. For ten years, she had a continuing nightmare about being chased by a monster which made her wake up, screaming. The monster was a disguised memory of Lynda being molested as a child, a pain Lynda had pushed away for years. As repeated knocks at Lynda's door, the nightmares said: You are emotionally crippled, get help; you need to face the pain and deal with it, so that you can love again.

Distinguishing True Warnings from Metaphors

When a message is important, dreams work hard to get your attention; and terrifying images get your attention. Covered as a full chapter in this book, nightmare

In a Nutshell:
The Main Points about Nightmares

You Are the Source. All dreams and nightmares, emerge from the dreamer's mind and soul as messages that arrive with a helpful purpose.

Specific Issues. Though nightmares feel bad, when decoded they hold a positive message to guide you through a specific obstacle. As you deal with the fear, anxiety, or challenge, the bad dreams disappear.

Exceptions. Though most nightmares deal with personal distress, the exceptions noted below are more than meets the eye, as covered in a later chapter.

* *Nightmares as a Genuine Warning.* On rare occasions, a nightmare is a true warning about an impending danger, challenge, or disaster.

* *Nightmares of Sensitive Souls.* Those with more sensitive personalities, such as artists, creative people, nurturers, and caregivers, sometimes suffer from frequent and persistent nightmares. At times, heartfelt attunement and sensitivity spill out as a nightmare.

* *Trauma and Nightmares.* Extreme trauma—such as combat, prolonged abuse, or surviving a natural disaster like a terrorist attack, hurricane, earthquake, flood, or fire—can create intense nightmares. In this extreme-nightmare form, the person relives the trauma nightly as nightmares that often bring sleep deprivation and ratchet distress levels up to extreme heights.

warnings that cite a life-and-death issue are rare. Most often, a nightmare targets issues that are urgent but not life-threatening, at least not yet. A scary image of an elevator-crash can mirror someone's downward tailspin due to alcohol or drugs. A skull and crossbones on food or a scowling doctor can be a heads-up about a health issue. A car crash can mirror arguments in a relationship that are coming to a head. An avalanche can be a hint about news that feels overwhelming, like the loss of a job or of a loved one who is ill. As a critical feature of nightmares, several upcoming chapters cover dream warnings of actual dilemmas and the messages that nightmares unveiled.

DREAMS, NIGHTMARES, THE MIND, AND THE PSYCHE: WHO IS RUNNING THE SHOW?

To understand nightmares and dreams, it helps to look at how the mind works. The psyche is defined here as the part of your awareness that oversees the body, mind, and, for believers, the soul—whether you are awake or asleep. The psyche is the general manager; it knows all and keeps all on track. As Freud and Jung pointed out, the mind is not a one-room apartment: the mind is a multi-story building that includes:

* *The awake you* who lives your day and goes to sleep at night.

* *The unconscious* as the autopilot which carries out automatic tasks like breathing, and complex tasks like driving, without having to concentrate on every detail. You notice the unconscious as daydreaming and unplanned mind lapses into the past or future. The unconscious is the autopilot that takes over during sleep, allowing awareness to continue as a night-light version.

* *Memory* is the storage bin of the mind.

* *The soul* is the source of inspiration, motivation, and faith.

* *The superconscious,* some surmise, may be a DNA awareness in your bones that connects all people, seen in our similar needs, survival instincts, and universal reactions, in all nations, like identical responses to smiles. Mystics view the superconscious as awareness beyond the norm that connects all creatures, all humanity, God, and what lies beyond.

The Psyche Connects the Dots

Here is a closeup of how the psyche works in relation to dreams and dreaming.

You Live Two Lives. During daily activities, you have different roles in the world, as a professional, a parent or sibling, a friend, a blogger, or an arts-and-crafts or wine connoisseur. In your second life, you engage in a secret, ongoing inner dialogue of thoughts and feelings about yourself and everything around you. The psyche mediates these inner and outer parts.

The Real You. The psyche is the "me" that defines you. It blends your inner thoughts, feelings, and hopes with your outer roles and interactions with people.

Traffic Cop. The psyche is the traffic cop that filters thoughts and feelings. At any given moment, you concentrate on what is important, yet there is a lot more going on around you than you take in. As you focus, the psyche screens out what is irrelevant.

Balancing Actions with Feelings and Thoughts. As you plow through your day, the psyche revs up your mind, logic, and intellect. At the same time, it has access to the unconscious, unaware parts of you that can bubble over as a sudden urge, thought, or feeling. When inner and outer parts are in balance, you feel whole and creative. We compliment someone who is in balance by saying they've got it together. When a person's outer roles and feelings are not in synch, you sense something odd about that person.

The Hub. If awareness was a wheel, the psyche would be the center hub that connects the spokes. It mediates roles, feelings, and thoughts with the goals and standards that you live by.

Reaching for More. Sometimes you reach out for spiritual answers beyond the daily norm, or ask for grace to get through a rocky patch. As a gateway to deeper levels, the psyche may connect you to your soul, to guardian angels, and, at times, to the divine itself. Some might see the psyche's connection to the soul as your inner voice.

The Psyche as a Built-In Counselor

As the interface between you and the world, the psyche has direct access to an entire lifetime of your thoughts, feelings, actions, and memories. As you sleep, the psyche reviews what happened during the day and compares the day's events to your ideals, goals, and hopes; after an in-depth review, by morning the psyche cranks out insights about the previous day's concerns and forwards insights as a dream message. Later chapters examine this powerful, built-in counselor function of the psyche, as seen in nightmares.

CHAPTER TWO

Analyze a Dream in Minutes

Because I have analyzed my dreams since I was nineteen, I know dreams pack a giant punch as a daily, built-in personal adviser. Dreams resolve problems, unveil others' motives and thoughts, point out talents and obstacles, and pick you up when you feel down. Getting insight from dreams is like hopping a ride in a luxury car instead of riding the streets on a rusty old bicycle: you'll reach your destination faster, safer, and in comfort. Ditch the bike and join the Rolls Royce Dream Club with the Five-Step Method, which explains how to understand your dreams, in minutes. Yes, it is that easy! Once you successfully analyze a dozen of your own dreams, you may appreciate the advantage of a personal dream adviser.

Dream Analysis Hints

What Does This Dream Mean?—Is *Not* the Question. Dreams are a drama about activities, problems, feelings, and sagas that make up the colorful tapestry of daily life. Because dreams are about your life, the *real* question is "What about me or my life is this dream talking about?" As you decipher a dream, keep the focus on how the story connects to you and your life.

Look Both Ways. Dreams are a two-way street; how you approach dreams matters! Curiosity entices you to remember a dream. Enthusiasm energizes the psyche to communicate with you during sleep. An open heart paves a path to memories used as building blocks in dreams. As is true in all of life, attitude counts.

Driving Lessons—Practice Makes Perfect. Using the five-step dream technique is like taking driving lessons—almost anyone can learn if they want to. Like driving, there are useful rules of the road. Depending on your enthusiasm, you can analyze dreams in a few hours or slowly in weeks or months as you explore dream messages. Dream analysis gets easier with practice. As you crack the code of one dream, the next one is easier to zone into. Regular dream analysis creates an instinctive understanding that gets stronger over time. When ready, your psyche may present deep insights that can surprise and enchant.

Dream Analysis as Play. Understanding dreams works best when you stay relaxed. Though dreams handle serious questions, a light, detached attitude invokes your creative side and enhances the ability to find the treasure. The psyche has a sense of humor; look for occasional dreams that poke fun and enjoy the journey. *Bonus Hint:* If you're curious about what is possible on the dream landscape, find a copy of *The Bedside Guide to Dreams* by Stase Michaels, which outlines twenty-seven dream types that you can experience.

FIRST GLANCE:
THE FIVE STEPS TO A DREAM MESSAGE

Let's start with a quick summary of the five-step method, followed by expanded sections that describe each, in detail.

1. *Emotions.* Notice what you feel during the dream, and as you wake up.

2. *Create a Story Line.* As if telling someone about a favorite movie, summarize the gist of the dream in one sentence. Focus on the actions, *but*—and this is important—use different words to restate what is going on as a *generalization*. Use words like "someone" and "something" to keep the description general. Take the example of a dream about a quarterback who fumbles a ball yet goes on to win the game. The story line could be: Someone messes up, yet recovers and succeeds brilliantly. Or: Someone loses a battle, yet wins the war. Both versions are one-liners, both are general statements that say nothing about football, a quarterback, or a fumble. Yet each version captures the gist of the story.

3. *Match the Story Line to an Area of Your Life.* The real question is always "What does the dream say about me or my life?" In step three, see how the story line fits into your life. What situations, thoughts, or feelings sound like the story? In the fumbled-football dream, ask: Where do I feel like I failed? Or: What challenge could I overcome, even if the odds seem impossible?

4. *Symbols.* Whether it is a person or an object, take a symbol and see what it reminds you of in your personal experience. In the football dream, a fan may relate football to their career, because they once

hoped to play professional football; a fumbled ball could relate to a missed opportunity for advancement. To a woman who is not a sports fan, football may remind her of an ex who loved the game, which reminds her of the divorce that left her feeling like a failure. Once the symbol brings up a memory, see how thoughts and feelings about the memory add to the story and its potential message.

5. *Use the Message.* The point of dream analysis is to get the message and use it. In the football dream, inspired by the successful dream ending, the man could get more training and be ready for the next round of promotions. For the woman, the football dream can be a heads-up that even though a marriage failed, the "game" of romance does not have to be over. And, encouraged that one can recover from a fumble, she might try again.

THE FIVE-STEP TECHNIQUE: HOW EACH STEP WORKS, WITH EXAMPLES

Once you get the rhythm, the five steps can zoom you straight to the heart of a dream message.

Step 1: Emotions

As examples show, dreams can help you name emotions and digest them, which can happen in a variety of ways.

Name That Feeling. When you are confused, in pain, or overwhelmed by a busy lifestyle, at times you may put feelings aside and store them on a back shelf. That works for a while, though a time arrives when you need to own those feelings. Like a game of Ping-Pong between the conscious and unconscious parts of the mind, the psyche knows when it is time to move pushed-away feelings back into your inbox. As an unhappy office worker, Jen soldiered on through boring work days. One night she dreamed she was riding on a bus, sitting next to a sad young woman who looked like her. Normally a happy camper, Jen realized that she was the sad girl who was feeling blue. Jen named her emotional state, owned it, and turned it around. Some dreams simply help you put a label on a feeling so that you can deal with it.

Digesting Feelings and Reactions. Intense fear, distress, and anxiety can shove your emotions off a cliff. Like a nighttime digestion system, dreams let you act out extreme emotions as a way to rebalance them. Jordan, an ambitious young man, was furious because his boss passed him over for a coveted project. In a dream, Jordan watched himself punch his boss in the face with angry, vicious blows. It felt good, until he bloodied his boss's face. Since he was normally kind and good-natured, the violent dream-pummeling spooked Jordan; even while dreaming, he knew his reactions were over the top. Waking up frightened, Jordan faced the truth. His boss was right: he did not have the seniority necessary to work on the project, and there would be other opportunities in the future. Digesting emotions as you sleep explains why, at times, you go to bed feeling troubled yet wake up feeling at peace. Even if a situation is not yet resolved—and even if you do not remember your dreams or analyze them later—thanks to this automatic digestion system, you can wake up feeling better.

Unplugging an Emotional Sink. When you are stuck in an emotional rut, the psyche can concoct a dream that precipitates a strong reaction in you, on purpose, as a shove in the right direction that gets you out of the rut. A blast of intense emotion in a dream can jolt you out of a complacent attitude in a relationship, or revive enthusiasm for an unused talent. A common example is a dream about having sex, where you make passionate love with someone that you despise. Yet it makes you feel great. When you wake up, you see the person differently; you cannot help yourself. The mutual pleasure created a positive bond and, like unplugging a sink, the bad feelings you had toward the person change. Negative feelings you hold on to like resentment, anger, or hatred can turn into a psychological boomerang that undermines your emotional well-being. When that happens, the psyche may create a dream to help you break away.

Chill Out. A dream can mirror how your bad moods or reactions make you look. John was a great guy with an easygoing nature—except when someone was late in a carpool that he shared with other dads, coordinating rides to take their kids to practice. If kids were late, John took it out on their fathers, leading to conversations with ugly sarcasm and condescension. One night he had a dream about a favorite childhood story, "The Ugly Duckling," that his grandmother read to him as a child. John loved the part at the end, where the rejected duck turns into a swan. In the dream, instead of becoming a swan, the ugly duckling turned in a mean, quacking beast that pecked at sibling ducklings, venting his frustrations with anger. Waking up, John was horrified, and shared the dream with his wife; she connected the dots and laughed. His wife had been listening to John's rants about late kids, hoping his impatience would pass. Seeing himself with new eyes, John chilled out during carpool rides. A scary dream can inspire you to return to your better self.

Feelings during a dream, as well as reactions just after you wake up, can be a pivotal clue to a dream message.

How You Feel When You Wake Up. Notice whether what you feel matches the story. If you see yourself in a coffin yet feel happy, the dream is not a forecast of death. Jacinta felt exhausted as she worked her way through college; one night she was shocked by a dream. She saw her body getting pulverized into paste, like pastry dough, then rolled out and cut by a giant cookie cutter, into a body-shaped chicken nugget. Then the nugget was deep-fried. As she woke up, the scene felt gory and terrifying. However, Jacinta soon realized that during the dream she felt content—she loved chicken nuggets! Feeling content in the dream was a major clue. The story describes someone who is taken apart, reshaped, and turned into something crispy that they love—chicken nuggets. The dream said: Though college is challenging, the experience will transform you and bring a tasty, happy life. What a great metaphor for going to college!

More or Less. Notice if a dream shows feelings that you have often, or emotions you could use more of. Quiet and shy in real life, Oscar saw himself in a dream, bravely demanding a raise from his boss. The dream invited him to be more assertive.

New or Surprising. Feeling surprised can signal a special message. If you see yourself win a race you did not know you had entered, or a slim version of yourself even though you haul around a few extra pounds, the message can be a special heads-up. Though happily married, Laurel was surprised by a dream of a high school sweetheart who made her laugh as they enjoyed an outdoor concert in a park. The joy she felt with the past beau was a sharp contrast to the blahs she secretly felt, at the time, with her husband. The dream reminded Laurel of what she really wanted. Hold on. The dream was not telling Laurel to look up the ex on social media. Instead, it was saying: To revive the romance you crave, do fun things with your husband, like you did when you were young. Ya think?

When surprise is a main feature of a dream, that feeling can signal new potentials or challenges. If the story line is positive, keep an antenna out for opportunities; if the story is scary or negative, look out for challenges. In a dream, Carl saw a brand-new car parked in his garage. Shocked and surprised, in the dream he told himself "I love it, but that can't be mine." The car was a model and color Carl craved in younger years, but by middle age had crossed off his bucket list. Was the dream a heads-up that someone would surprise him with that car? Nada. But a promotion a while later came with a fat new paycheck that allowed Carl to buy any car his heart desired. Content, Carl picked a less flashy model than the vehicle of his teenage fantasies.

A Dream Shock or Zinger. If a dream shakes you up or leaves you emotionally dazed or dazzled, your reaction may hold a hidden message or be an invitation to shift a perspective. Annie grew up on a farm, and as a child she loved the hens and chicks that scampered around the yard. Annie kept dreaming about a chicken that was trying to cross a busy highway; in each dream, she feared for the chicken's life and woke up in a cold sweat. It took a while for Annie to realize that *she* was the chicken trying to cross the road—as push was coming to shove in a downhill relationship with her alcoholic husband. For the sake of her children, Annie wanted to take charge of her life and leave, yet lacked the courage to strike out on her own. In the English language, if you are "a chicken," you are afraid. The frantic hen trying to cross the highway was an image of her bottled-up frustration about her marriage, and each time Annie watched the plucky chicken, she inhaled more and more courage. In a final dream, when the chicken safely crossed the road, Annie knew it was time to pack her bags. Nightmare zingers helped Annie face a challenge and, when ready, to embark on a better life.

Step 2: The Story Line

Hints: Story-Line Ins and Outs. The story line is a single sentence that states the gist of the dream—*but . . . in generalities.* The story line unveils the secret that's hidden in the obvious. Here's the scoop on how to do a story line:

1. *Capture the Essence of the Action.* As you summarize the dream, focus on actions. A dream about training long hours for the

Olympics and winning a medal could have the following story line: Hard work brings great success. Or: Someone persists and achieves an outstanding goal.

2. *Use Generalities.* Do not repeat the actual names of objects or people: instead, paraphrase the story with words like "someone" or "something." Like a silhouette, generalities eliminate details to reveal the big picture and overall direction. A woman who loves shoes dreams that she is trying on a dozen pairs, and selects a pair of red high heels that look amazing. The story line could be: Someone examines what fits and selects something dramatic, which suits them. There is no mention of a woman, shoes, or the color red, yet the gist of the story is clear.

3. *Put Symbols on Hold.* Some approaches in dream analysis ask you to immediately focus on the characters and symbols, but doing this can create a distraction that leads you down the wrong path. Symbols and dream characters provide valuable information and deserve a spotlight. But not yet. Other than exceptions discussed in a later section on symbols, in most dreams symbols play a supporting role to the story line. Think of symbols as a spice that creates the "wow" factor to enhance the main meal. Leading with a story line lets you scout the territory, create a map, and avoid jumping to conclusions, which is the most common error in dream analysis.

Connie dreamed she was riding a Ferris wheel, almost fell off, yet kept her balance and then enjoyed the ride. The dream scared her, even though it felt good to hold on. Connie had a fear of heights and hated going to Fairs. In real life, Connie had been invited to a family reunion that was going to be held at a local fairground. At first, the

Ferris wheel and fairground, as negative associations for her, inclined Connie to say no. Yet the story line said "Someone prevails in an unsteady situation," which sounded more like encouragement for Connie to hang on and overcome her fears. Connie realized that she loved her large family, and, reminded of her strengths by that dream, resolved to attend.

4. *Stand Back.* Sometimes, as soon as you wake up from a dream, you think you know what it means. Maybe you do—or maybe you don't. Experience suggests it can be wise to step back for a second and pretend you do not know what the dream means, at least not yet. Start with a story line and mentally run through the five steps; doing so might dramatically alter a first impression. To avoid jumping to conclusions, create a story line before you commit to what a dream means.

Story Lines for Long Dreams

A long dream can be a message with several parts to it; or can be several dreams, in sequence, that feel like a single dream. Here are a few tips for creating a story line when a dream is extra-long.

1. *Create a Story Line for Each Segment.* Separate a long dream into its natural parts and give each part its own story line. Read the story lines in sequence to see if they add up to an overall picture about an issue, or whether each story line points to a separate issue.

2. *Mini-Themes.* Sometimes a long dream is a disjointed maze of actions or people making it hard to fathom a meaningful story line. Instead of a story line, look for mini-themes like "running away" or "looking

for something" or "trying to feel safe." You can also try to spot similarities, differences, or opposites such as love versus hate, or acting silly versus acting serious—which can be turned into a story line, or used as a theme, instead of a story line. When a mini-theme runs through several segments, let it be a story line. *Bonus Hint:* If several opposites appear such as good versus evil, or cowardly versus brave, it is often a message about the need to find balance on that topic.

3. *Story Lines in a Long Dream—As Variations on an Issue.*

* *Similar Points.* Segments in a long dream can make similar points on a single issue. For a person with low confidence, three segments may mirror a low self-esteem or show stories that inspire confidence.

* *An Overview.* A long dream can be an overview. The first part may summarize the past; the next, mirror the present; and a third point to the future, on a topic.

* *Variations on a Theme.* A long dream can give several variations on an issue to expand your understanding. One part may show how a childhood situation affected the topic; another, how your current feelings play a part; and a third hint how others see the issue.

Step 3: Match the Story Line to Life

Story Line: A Life Compass. When starting out, try two or three variations of a story line. Once a story line captures the thrust of a dream, it becomes a compass that leads to the message. Like trying on a pair of shoes, see how the story fits your life. Does it match feelings, thoughts, ideas, or goals? Does it match an activity, a relationship, or an overall situation? If the matchup to your life is not obvious, try a few questions. A dream about running a race and winning a gold medal can have

Classic Techniques to Determine What a Symbol Means

You can ponder the meaning of a dream symbol as you sip a cup of coffee, take a walk, or while stuck in traffic. Try these techniques. They work!

The Association Method

A classic approach to vetting a symbol is Sigmund Freud's association method. Pick a symbol that resonates and see what memory comes up about the image. Note whether the memory relates to the story. Take another step backward: use that memory to find a new, related one and see if the new memory sheds light on the dream. As in the following example, keep working backward until something clicks; an "aha" can jump out at the first, second, or third pass.

As a high school senior, Brad had a recurring nightmare about a grizzly bear that jumps out of nowhere. Just as the bear is about to attack, it spots a nearby beehive, stops in its tracks, and dashes off to get some honey. Though Brad escapes, he woke up terrified. Brad was applying to a college whose high standards had him in a sweat; he guessed the nightmare was about college anxieties. Lying back on his pillow, Brad was intrigued by the honey and beehive symbols. Suddenly Brad remembered a favorite bedtime story, *Winnie the Pooh*, and a favorite passage that said, "You are braver than you believe, stronger than you seem, and smarter than you think." Brad felt tears trickle down his cheek. His dad read the story to him as a child, in between his dad's tours of duty as a combat soldier; they had buried his dad as a war hero when Brad was twelve. Brad could hear his father's voice saying he was brave, strong, and smart. As symbols, the bear and the honey uncovered Brad's secret bedtime exchange with his father. Thanks to the unearthed memories, as Brad faced college and life as a young man, his confidence soared.

The Amplification Method

Psychologist Carl Jung coined the term "amplification" for dream symbols. Instead of going backward in memory, Jung listed his current thoughts about a symbol. In a dream about baseball, someone hits the ball so hard that the bat splits. Instead of wondering when you last saw a baseball game or played, notice what baseball means to you. Baseball can represent a warm summer day, the outdoors, having fun as a kid. You can also note emotions about baseball like feeling relaxed, a love of sports, the warmth of a close family. Consider how each association relates to your dream. Is baseball a metaphor about a need to relax or spend time with family? Does the split bat reference a fence that needs mending? As personal symbols and memories, only you, the dreamer, know the answers.

Fritz Perls: Become the Dream Symbol

Sometimes an intense dream leaves you stumped! If that happens, explore your feelings about the dream. How? Psychiatrist Fritz Perls encouraged dreamers to "become" a dream character." You can have an imagined written conversation between you and a dream symbol. Or, whether alone or as a group activity, you can act out the symbol by placing two chairs face to face. One is you, the other, the dream character. It sounds nutty but as you move back and forth between chairs and act out each role, remarkable insights can unfold. Becoming a dream symbol works for intense dreams and when logic fails to grasp a message. Known as *gestalt*, the technique plugs you into your intuitive, unconscious mind; feelings emerge that catapult you to the heart of a message. When all else fails or even just for fun, become the dream symbol! Instead of an example, take this challenge. Select an intense dream image, become the symbol, and see what happens!

the story line "Through effort and persistence, someone achieves an amazing goal." Questions can be "What would I love to accomplish that takes effort and persistence?" or "Do I have a goal that feels beyond my reach that I should persist with?" Once you match an area of life to the story, a message often clicks.

Once in a while, an attempt to line up the story with your life comes up blank. If a new version of the story line, with generalized words, still does not fit, put the dream aside; perspectives shift over time. There are other possibilities. Although most dreams are about you, sometimes a dream is not about you; the message can be about a loved one. Or the dream can be about a future event, so the story line does not fit what you are experiencing now. Keep an eye on dreams that do not fit; they can be important. The answer often unfolds, in time.

Step 4: Symbols: Snatches from Memories and Associations

Symbols relate to personal memories. A word to the wise: Leave the dream dictionary and its cookie-cutter approach to dream interpretation in the pantry. Dream dictionaries pop up everywhere because they sound like an easy fix. However, a dream dictionary cannot tell you what a symbol really means, because . . . the true meaning is unique to you—and only you! Five people can dream of a red rose, yet the rose means something different to each person. To one woman, a rose is a reminder of love as the flower her husband presented to her every Valentine's Day. To another dreamer, roses are a reminder of death and loss as a red bouquet on their loved one's coffin. For a third person, a rose represents patience, the blossom that is hardest to cultivate in their garden. And so on. Knowing what a symbol means is simple; check your memories about what the symbol means to you. As a word, association is about linking a dream symbol to a memory of an actual person, scene, or object, in your life.

The Mechanics of a Dream Symbol

In the game of charades, you act out a phrase without saying words, like pointing a finger at an ear to say "sounds like." Charades gives a silent visual clue about objects that leads to another meaning, about a song or movie title. The same happens with dream symbols: a metaphor is a visual "stand-in" for a second meaning. Like a game of charades, the psyche presents an image and invites you to translate the image into a related, metaphoric meaning. Someone browsing through a box of mementos can be a metaphor for "going back in time," asking you to note something from your past. Like charades, images that your psyche selects for a dream message are not random; each is picked because of a memory link to something that highlights a message. Think of dream symbols as a game of charades and dive fearlessly into your treasure chest of memories.

Symbols Mirror How You Communicate

Notice how you communicate. As it cranks out a dream, the psyche mimics how you express yourself. A polite dreamer tends to have polite dream characters. Someone who is emotional and poetic has flowery dream scenes, filled with detail. The dreams of a direct person of few words can pack a lot of meaning into a short story, with few symbols. Dreams mirror your communication style. Be you. Do you.

Have No Fear—You Already Speak the Symbol's Language

Understanding a dream symbol is as natural as getting the punch line of a joke. Review your memories about a dream person or object. Sift what those memories mean to you and how they may apply to the dream story. Notice your emotional reactions to a symbol, now and in the past. As you explore such associations, you quickly become an expert about your symbols and metaphors.

Symbols add flavor. In step three, you match a story line to your life and often, at this point, you may get the drift of a dream message. But wait, there's more! Before you add symbols to the mix, the message is like a plain bagel or a cake with no icing. As a pinch of deeper insight, symbols add flavor to a message. Jordan dreamed that he punched his boss in the face and enjoyed himself in the dream, until he drew blood. The bloody face was an association rooted in memory for Jordan, who felt the connection to a childhood incident at a family gathering where a drunk uncle, to everyone's horror, hit his wife and bloodied her nose. To Jordon, a bloody face said: Your anger is way out of line. The unmasked memory link to a bloody face in his childhood made the message more potent. A story line is ruled by the head; a symbol touches emotions and adds a "wow" moment on impact. Take the time to unlock the hidden meaning of symbols and unleash your own OMG's and wow's.

Symbols can repeat. Sometimes the same symbolic link can echo through a dream several times. A scene representing Olympic training can include a five-mile run, a bike ride, and a hundred push-ups—or even more. Each exercise is a repeated refrain indicating persistence and pushing oneself to the limit. Repetition adds emphasis to the dream, like an exclamation point!

Symbols can amp the message up. Like a pungent spice, a symbol can add an unexpected zing to a dream message. A past memory link can sharply alter your perspective on a message, like adding the distinct flavor of chocolate or lemon to a batter, which steers the result in a particular direction.

For all these reasons, symbols are an important item in the psyche's toolbox.

Step 5: The Dream Message

Once you know what a dream means, there is a final step. When you ask a friend for advice, they expect you to consider their input. As a deeper part of you, the psyche is a voice of your better angels that communicates what you should do or be, to bring out the best in yourself. Own this quiet, inner voice and dream guidance. Apply it and make it work for you.

As practical and constructive messages, a dream may invite you to adopt a new attitude, change your approach in a relationship, dare you to try a new activity, or encourage you to cope with a challenge. Whatever the message, apply it in a manner consistent with who you are, where you are at, and where your life is heading. Used correctly, dream advice creates a series of natural, positive, forward steps. Unless a dream is a warning about a life-and-death issue, a message rarely turns your life upside down or suggests a drastic change that you didn't see coming. Balanced, natural steps are the way to go.

APPLYING THE FIVE-STEP METHOD: THREE EXAMPLES

NIGHTMARE

The Five-Step Method, Example #1:
No Place to Shower

Amelia was a senior advertising executive. She dreamed she was both a doctor and a businesswoman. In the dream, Amelia had a pet koala bear that she dropped off at company headquarters for safekeeping while she completed a project. When her work was done, Amelia retrieved the cuddly Australian bear and went home. She looked for a place to shower because, in her dream role as a doctor, she had to prepare for surgery. Amelia couldn't find a shower. She was staying at a luxury hotel which should have had showers, but when she checked with the manager, he confirmed there were no showers. Baffled and frustrated, Amelia settled for a quick wash.

Story Line: Frustrated that a normal amenity is not available, someone accepts a superficial facsimile.

Feelings: Distress in the dream; puzzled on awakening.

Relevance: Amelia had just finished a year-long project and desperately wanted a vacation. However, she was immediately offered a new project; it was both a step forward and something she wanted. Amelia wanted a month-long vacation yet had to start the new project right away, which created a conflict between her head and her emotions—as a push–pull that the dream addressed.

Key Symbols:

KOALA BEAR: Something lovable and unusual that defined how Amelia felt about her career and the new assignment.

PREPARING FOR SURGERY: A surgeon performs a critical service that helps others. The image hinted that the new assignment was important, which was in line with the dreamer's ideal of wanting to help others.

A SHOWER: A place to cleanse and be refreshed; a metaphor in this dream of a vacation, a desire to be refreshed between major assignments.

A QUICK WASH: A metaphor about taking a short break instead taking a full vacation.

Analysis: The dream reminded Amelia that the new opportunity would help others, which was her goal. Amelia shifted perspectives, took a short break, and felt at peace with the new assignment.

The Five-Step Method, Example #2:
Mother in Handcuffs

In the second example, Denise was an unemployed 50-year-old whose mom had just died. As she sorted out her late mother's belongings, Denise had a nightmare, where she saw her mother lying on a bed, handcuffed, wailing softly. Shocked at her mother's condition, Denise keeps trying to reassure her mother. Feeling frantic, Denise tells her mom that her eldest brother has been told what is going on, and is on his way to help.

Story Line: Someone sees a loved one in a painful and limited situation and assures them that all will be well.

Feelings: Very sad; kept wanting to reassure mother.

Relevance: The story mirrored how Denise felt.

Key Symbols:

HANDCUFFS: Extreme limitations.

MOTHER, DECEASED MOTHER: Someone who nurtures and protects; in this dream, a symbol of nurturing yet loss. Metaphor of what dreamer wants, a job, but lost.

WAILING: An expression of pain; a cry for help.

ELDEST BROTHER: Symbolized dreamer's own strength that she was reaching for.

Analysis: The older brother was a symbol of strength that Denise had, but could not yet get into gear. Words spoken in a dream often hold the message. The reassurance that Denise gave her mom was a message of reassurance to herself that help was on the way, in the form of her own strength, to which she would reconnect. In the guise of an older brother who was coming to the rescue his little sister, Denise reminded herself she had the strength to cope and turn things around.

Uplifted, Denise responded: "Thank you! And God Bless."

NIGHTMARE

The Five-Step Method, Example #3:
On Fire

The Dreamer: Juliana was a forty-something math teacher with a heart of gold, who loved teaching. Still single, she was outgoing in the classroom, yet reserved in personal relationships. The years were catching up. Juliana decided to explore how to express her feelings; she read books, took seminars, and had conversations with those she trusted.

> One night Juliana had a nightmare. In the dream, she was watching a documentary about geometry; the screen showed animated, geometric figures dashing around on a red background. But something was wrong with the CD or the player and suddenly it was on fire! Alarmed as she saw the fire on screen, Juliana woke up, terrified.

Story Line: Something contained and predictable turns into an out-of-control situation that can create problems.

Feelings: Frightened, troubled, had the thought: "Somebody's trying to tell me something."

Relevance: Mirrors Juliana's exploration about feelings.

Key Symbols:

WATCHING A DOCUMENTARY: What someone is trying to learn.

THE COLOR RED: Often a symbol of danger.

GEOMETRIC FIGURES: Orderly, predictable and contained objects, like dreamer's emotions.

FIRE: A two-edged sword. When controlled, a useful tool (heat or cooking); when out of control, can be destructive. In this dream, a metaphor about emotions.

Analysis: In a sense, Juliana was the CD and the CD player—she was both the source and the controller of geometric images and actions, as metaphors of her feelings. Watching the figures catch on fire terrified Juliana, pointing to fears that if she showed emotions, they could get out of control. Juliana was afraid to loosen her grip on feelings in case they got out hand. The nightmare did not say anything bad would happen. The message simply said: "Bravo, you are exploring your emotions. But first, notice how afraid you are of expressing your feelings." To get it right, Juliana first had to own a hidden fear that went along with taking a deeper look at herself.

Juliana said: "Thank you! I thought the dream was saying—this is dangerous, stop! It was a relief to read nothing bad will happen as I feel and examine my emotions. So true, I need to work on this."

Bonus Hint: Dreaming is a very safe way to get in touch with your true feelings. And as this dream shows, one important function of dreams is to put you in touch with feelings you may not be aware of.

For more examples of the five-step method in action for nightmares and other dreams, check out the online library of dreams at Interpretadream.com.

CHAPTER THREE

Nightmares That Digest Fears and Anxieties

When you feel safe and loved, you tend to have good dreams. The opposite is also true. During a crisis, fear and anxiety brings nightmares as a side-effect of turmoil. That is why the author says that, for the most part, there are no frightening dreams—only frightened dreamers. There is good news. A nightmare is the equivalent of a talk with a friend about a serious problem, a friend who knows you well and has your best interests at heart. Even if a nightmare shakes you up, like all dreams, its message generally offers a solution. The next time you have a nightmare, set fear aside and look for the message.

FEAR GIVES BIRTH TO NIGHTMARES

Like a car that spins out of control, intense fear or anxiety can unbalance perceptions and feelings. When you are in turmoil, normal dream images that usually carry a constructive message instead do a somersault and don a scary disguise. When you put a tree branch underwater, the branch looks rippled and uneven; water distorts what is beneath the surface. A friendly pup trotting down a dark street at midnight looks terrifying at a distance. In the same way, a normal dream that is distorted by fear or anxiety is experienced as a nightmare.

Amahle had regular nightmares about trying to defend her five-year-old wheelchair-bound son from attacking tigers. In real life, Amahle was sleep-deprived as she struggled to protect her special-needs son from insensitive words and actions. Though Amahle had courage, her daily battle created a stress overload that spilled over into nightmares. Amahle discovered a support group for moms with special-needs children; once she embraced their support and began to get more sleep, the nightmares vanished. Wait, not so fast. What really vanished were Amahle's fears about being able to meet her child's needs.

Like attending a Halloween party, normal dream images can put on a scary costume as a masking or dark-cloak effect. . . . If everyone was as trusting as an innocent child and could accept that all dreams are there to help, no dream would turn into a nightmare. But as mere humans, fear, distress, and anxiety creep in and lead to nightmares. As you engage dreams in a positive and fearless manner, the dark-cloak effect softens.

NIGHTMARES AND STRESS—THEN AND NOW

Nightmares are the most requested dreams for analysis on the author's website, Interpretadream.com. Nightmares are about stress; and how we experience stress has changed dramatically. Before the world was swallowed by a giant electronic whale called the Internet, the big issues for many were births, deaths, accidents, dog bites, burglaries, and a small helping of politics. Today that is no longer true: the world is now a giant village whose hourly crises blast onto our digital screens, large and small. Television shows like *Game of Thrones* may leave some wondering if today's stress is simply different, though not less, than a few hundred years ago, but that is a moot question. Sixty years ago, your age, neighborhood, and economic and social background defined you. The Internet is an amazing social leveler, which has its merits—yet the electronic age also amps up our collective stress, which in turn ratchets up our collective potential for nightmares.

RESEARCH EXPLAINS THE RESTORATIVE POWER OF SLEEP AND DREAMS

Thanks to a groundbreaking study by Lulu Zie, et al. (*Science*, 2013 Oct 18, 342:6156), science now explains why you feel refreshed after a good night's sleep. During each sleep stage, including the dreaming phase, which is called REM (rapid eye movement) sleep, the brain performs a nightly cleanup of "neurotoxic wastes" that accumulate from daily stress, toxins, and bacteria. John McKinley and fellow researchers put it this way: sleep is a rebalancing function that the brain carries out to clear toxic, metabolic byproducts in the brain, which we accumulate while awake (*Science*, 342:10.1126).

When you sleep, the brain reorganizes and recharges itself by removing toxic waste. In their review of the topic, Andy Eugene and Jolanta Masiak suggest a few bonus effects related to this nightly cleansing. The nightly cleanup not only clears the brain to help maintain normal brain function; the clean-up also relieves stress and depression, helps prolong memory, and aids in mental alertness

(*MedTube Sci.* 2015 Mar, 3/1:35–40). This amazing, nightly janitorial function of the brain happens automatically, and works best when you get enough sleep.

Extra-Credit Hint: Sleep and Alzheimer's Prevention

One of the most exciting aspects of this nightly brain cleanup relates to Alzheimer's. Research shows that plaque—the dreaded brain tangles seen in Alzheimer's—is scrubbed away as you sleep—during this neurological cleanup. All the more reason to get at least seven hours of sleep per night as the minimum recommended for a fully restorative sleep!

DREAMING AS AN ANTIDOTE TO STRESS

An important function of dreaming is to digest feelings that are out of kilter or are on overload. Do you ever go to sleep distressed, yet wake up feeling better? After a good night's sleep, something in you knows all is well and that a solution is on the horizon, even if you do not yet have the solution. Such rebalancing of feelings is part of the "emotional restoration function" that researchers Ramon Greenberg and Ernest Hartmann attribute to sleep and dreaming. It takes six to eight hours for normal nightly sleep cycles to sort out emotions; yet an epidemic number of people admit that they do not get enough sleep. As a default house-keeping system, dreaming is the equivalent of a built-in software of the mind that rebalances stress and maintains psychological health. This restorative aspect of dreaming is a remarkable gift that sleep offers—if you get enough sleep!

NIGHTMARES THAT HEAL EMOTIONS

When intense emotions make you feel as if you are riding a raging bull, dreams and nightmares can help digest those feelings. When you do the following, you discover what the "emotional restoration function" of dreaming can look like.

Step Outside Yourself

A dream story uses fictional characters or familiar people as actors who are stand-ins for you, so most dreams are about you. Like a mirror, a dream character portrays your feelings or flags what is amiss in your emotional make-up. In psychological terms, a dream lets you externalize feelings into a visible story, outside yourself. When we are awake, we tend to run from painful feelings; as we sleep, the day's emotions and pain re-surface and mirrored in a dream. During a dream, you distance yourself from intense or hidden feelings and by doing so, a problem or emotion becomes easier to spot and handle.

Label Those Feelings

Before you can deal with an emotion, you have to correctly name it. Watching others act out your emotions in a dream empowers you to recognize, flag, and label what you feel.

Trends

Like all dreams, nightmares include hints about how to cope with what ails you. At first you may not notice the suggestion. Look closely. A dream can show that you're on a harrowing journey, and despite many perils, the ending reveals that you do reach your destination. Reaching a destination is a hint that a solution is on its way. If you do not reach your destination yet survive, the message invites you to hone your strengths, persevere, and keep going.

Look Closely at the Characters in Your Nightmare

The characters in your nightmares can demonstrate a solution. Augustin, whose home is in South Africa, had a nightmare about a lion that showed up in his backyard and was about to attack. When Augustin ran into his house and locked the door, the lion left. Locking the door mirrored a need to feel secure, and it can be a metaphor about setting boundaries. People and circumstances can intrude on personal boundaries, which can feel like an attack. Locking a door is a hint about setting limits.

Look for Hints at the End of a Nightmare

Laura was a mother grieving over the traumatic loss of a stillborn baby. In a nightmare, she and her husband are driving. Suddenly, a hole opens up in the sky and a tornado appears. Laura's husband tells her they must drive into the open portal. The message, embedded in the dream ending, says: The only way out is through. Dreams help digest painful emotions; but when the wound is deep, it can take time.

NIGHTMARES THAT HANDLE STRESS

Nightmares often confront a dreamer's stress, as in this example.

NIGHTMARE

The Car Accident

The Dreamer: Aisha and her husband lived an ideal life; he had a great job, she loved being a stay-at-home mom of three kids. When her husband lost his job, Aisha felt overwhelmed with stress. Her children needed a lot for a new school year, and Aisha was plagued by a fear that they could lose their home. However, as a good wife, she pushed her fears away and tried to reassure her family that all would be well. However, a nightmare left her screaming, terrified, and shaking.

Aisha dreamed that she and her husband were driving on the freeway when a car flipped in front of them and landed on top of their car, shattering their windshield. The driver and passenger in the other car were dead. Aisha woke up wondering if the dream announced another tragedy.

Story Line: A sudden, unexpected, confrontation creates terrible consequences, which relates to Aisha's fears and distress about finances.

Key Symbols:

DRIVING ON HIGHWAY: Daily life, going forward on the road of life.

A CAR FLIPS: What turns over; metaphor for life that has turned upside down.

VEHICLE LANDS ON YOU: A crash; a sudden, unexpected tragedy.

SHATTERED WINDSHIELD: A shattered view, life feels shattered.

DEATH: Death as change, a metaphor of the painful changes in the dreamer's life.

Analysis: Most dreams are symbolic and death tends to be a metaphor about change, often an unpleasant or sudden change. Aisha's nightmare mirrored the shock she felt when confronted with extreme financial challenges. The out-of-control car spoke of overwhelmed emotions: life felt out of control as Aisha took a horrible ride, feeling as helpless as dead weight, like the dead passenger. In the dream, Aisha feels fear. The stress was too much to handle during the day, so, like a nighttime digestion system, the psyche used scary images like an innoculation that allowed Aisha to face what she feared. Once she felt the fear and named it, she could find her strength, and let fear subside. It can take time to feel stronger; digestion nightmares are there to help.

CHAPTER FOUR

NIGHTMARES THAT CONFRONT YOU ABOUT YOU!

Nightmares can reveal dusty, hidden negatives. This chapter invites you to go eyeball to eyeball with nightmares that feature your limitations, negative characteristics, and warts, which we like to pretend do not exist. Except that they do. We are good at hiding our less-than-perfect traits from ourselves. A temper that easily ignites is obvious to everyone except you. An inclination to hog attention can annoy the heck out of everyone, except you. Yet during times when life feels vulnerable, it can be okay to remain blind to your shortcomings, at least for a while. It takes confidence, strength, and maturity to face yourself full-on. There is no rush, though sooner or later we all have to face the music.

EMBRACE YOUR DARK SIDE

Once you dare to explore your shadows—and doing so does bring out the best in you—proceed without fear. Mystics say that knowing yourself is a crucial tool in spiritual advancement. *Bonus Hint:* Using dreams to quietly explore your deeper parts is a kick-ass way to get to fully know yourself—and to leap forward.

During sleep, you no longer control what you see or feel, so hints about negative parts of yourself can sneak into dreams. In *Star Wars*, Luke Skywalker comes face-to-face with Darth Vader; he is shocked to discover that his nemesis is his father, the man he has been seeking all his life. That is how it can feel to meet an unsavory part of yourself: it's scary, but when you do, you get a reward. Each slice of dark side that you redeem connects you to your authentic self, flaws and all, and unleashes a powerful new energy.

Hidden in every negative trait is a positive potential. The flip side of anger can be leadership. The flip side of depression can be the ability to inspire. The flip side of bullying can be unexpressed empathy and getting in touch with a need to be loved. When you face a negative and own it, you release its hidden positive. The opposite is also true: hiding from a negative trait can clog your potential; it takes a lot of energy to keep a secret fear or limitation at bay. As you accept yourself, flaws and all, your emotional toes can wade into a cool stream of unleashed talent and energy.

LOVE HURTS

Let's be real: the ego hates to face unpleasant truths. Studies in psychology confirm that we tend to inflate our opinions about ourselves, so a peek into a 360-degree mirror is an ordeal for anyone! Owning a weakness, any weakness, does not jive with the normal image we hold about ourselves, an image that says

"I am great and my life is in good shape." Yes, you are great, and sometimes your life is going well. Except that . . . most of us are a still work in progress.

Take the scene of a woman having lunch with friends, who shares some gossip. Someone laughs and calls her a bitch. Even if everyone laughs, the ego experiences the remark as a slap in the face. Taken aback, she feels misunderstood; all she did was tell a joke about someone's mishap, and so-and-so took it the wrong way. She knows she is good-natured, and she is. Except . . . sometimes she is a bitch too, which is hard to own up to.

When a nightmare implies that you are a bitch, a bully, or whatever, take a breath. The temporary ouch is a small price to pay for the transformation you can achieve. Though initially painful, nightmares that unmask your flaws are an act of kindness: they free you to be authentic. Don't push a nightmare's finger-wag away; instead, bring out the crystal glasses and champagne, and celebrate!

NIGHTMARE SELFIES: THREE LEVELS OF NIGHTMARES THAT INVITE YOU TO FACE YOURSELF

When a nightmare about a personal shortcoming jumps into your in-box, it can throw several kinds of punches your way—from light to hard—as the nightmare unmasks a hidden no-no, pain, or limitation. Let's begin with an overview of the three kinds of nightmares: stories that tread lightly, projections in nightmares, and nightmares that are morality tales. Detailed explanations follow, with examples of each type of "nightmare selfie."

Gentle Nightmare Selfies

Sometimes you feel vulnerable, yet your psyche has to deliver a painful message about you or where you are at. To ensure the message gets through, images that deliver the bad news or invite painful reflections may be less scary. Jeff was a high school student who prided himself on an ability to multitask. Each night, he spent a couple of hours doing homework, with the TV blasting in the background; Jeff was confident that the TV did not hinder his studies. Months later, when his math grades did not measure up, as a subject Jeff found challenging, he was inclined to blame his teacher. Jeff had a nightmare about a student at a computer, hounded by a swarm of mosquitoes. The story described an annoying distraction that interfered with what someone was doing. Oops. As a gentle punch, the mosquito-bite images were uncomfortable rather than terrifying. Motivated to get good grades, Jeff traded soft music, while doing homework. Pages 46–54 have more examples of Gentle Selfie nightmares.

Projection Nightmare—That Can't Be Me

Even when you know that you are off track, most people do not want to be confronted with their shortcomings and stubbornly resist a finger wag, even from their own dreams. When the psyche needs to point out an incorrect attitude or behavior to save you from yourself and resistance is in play, a dream may portray someone else acting out incorrect behavior. That is called projection: you easily accept others doing what you hide about yourself. Ethyl was a good-natured thirty-something office worker. In a nightmare, she saw her sister having a terrible tantrum in public. Her sister did have a short fuse, so it was easy for Ethyl to accept the scene, as in "Hey, bad sis, shame on you." News flash: As Ethyl quickly realized, the nightmare was a finger-wag at her, not at her sister. Ethyl had become short-tempered with an annoying a new colleague. Like the famous Trojan-horse caper in Greek history, the dream had sneaked in a believable decoy—her sister— which allowed the "You are a bad girl" message to slip through before Ethyl could say "That can't be me!" Yes, it can be me—and you—and all of us! Pages 56–69 have more examples of Projection nightmares.

Morality Issues—A Scary Story with an Underlying Moral

What you believe and what is important to you, defines you. The morals, standards, and ideals that you hold, and by which you measure your own actions, speak to the heart of your integrity and your ability to be authentic, whether or not others are watching. People and circumstances can intensely challenge what you believe, so it is not surprising that moral issues appear in nightmares.

A nightmare can be a morality tale with a message. We love a scary drama whose every twist and turn leads you, spellbound, toward an unexpected conclusion. Kim was a thirty-something who dreamed that she was being chased by a terrifying devil. The devil catches her arm. She fights, escapes, and runs frantically through a house, asking for help. But no one helps her, so Kim keeps running till she reaches a nearby woods, where she is alone, yet safe. Kim's life was filled with challenge, and no one was helping. In the nightmare, Kim struggles to survive by reaching out to others, but finds a safe space, all by herself. And that is the moral of the story. To break free from her troubles, depicted as a devil, and find her authentic, strong self, Kim had to learn to stand on her own two feet, not wait for friends, family, or Prince Charming to rescue her. Pages 70–75 have more examples of Morality nightmares.

GENTLE NIGHTMARE SELFIES

The previous overview was a glimpse into selfie nightmares. But wait, there's more. For the real gold, dig through a few examples.

When a nightmare wakes you up, you can feel terrified, raw, intense, and even unhinged for hours. During a nightmare gut punch, it can be hard to look for the message; however, finding one is worthwhile.

Gentle Selfie, Example #1:
An Assassin's Death Threat

The Dreamer: Charlotte was a lonely twenty-four-year-old, weighed down by a hundred extra pounds. Any time she left home, she felt great anxiety and feared that her weight could kill her.

> One night, Charlotte had a nightmare about a teenage assassin whose mission was to kill her; and during a violent struggle, the teen does almost kill her. Terrified, Charlotte woke up and could not go back to sleep, fearing the dream assassin could come back and she would actually die of something like a heart attack.

Analysis: The fight with the assassin mirrored a fierce struggle with weight that kept Charlotte from embracing life. Though unpleasant, the terror itself was a gentle wake-up call. As a paradox, the assassin mirrored Charlotte's strength, a fierceness in herself that she could call on, to create change. Charlotte worked through her vulnerable feelings and accepted the challenge to fight, survive, and reach out for the happiness that she longed for.

Gentle Selfie, Example #2:
I Am the Grim Reaper

The Dreamer: Isaiah was a manager in his family's grocery business, yet by age thirty-one he felt stifled.

> In a nightmare, Isaiah became the Grim Reaper, which shocked him. In his dream, an old lady who lived in a mansion kidnapped children

and turned them into slaves; giant spiders crushed any intruders. Isaiah had to rescue the children, but to do so Isaiah had to become the Grim Reaper, battle the spiders, and kill the old woman. Such acts were foreign to his gentle nature, but the children had to be rescued, so Isaiah carried out the task. He woke up feeling gratified, but also terrified and confused. Isaiah would never hurt anyone; the nightmare shook him up for days.

Analysis: It was a story about taking drastic steps to help others. Like death as a dream symbol, the Grim Reaper is often a metaphor about change, a change Isaiah wanted. Isaiah secretly longed to be a teacher, and the dream story mirrored a battle to be true to himself. Though the confrontation with himself felt scary, the gentle nightmare punch unleashed the impetus that Isaiah needed, to leave the family business and become a teacher.

NIGHTMARE

Gentle Selfie, Example #3:
Conversation with My Dead Father

The Dreamer: At age twenty-three, Cindy became a single mom with two young children she could barely support. Cindy was devastated.

The Nightmare—Told in the Dreamer's Own Words:

"It was a strange dream. In real life my mother is still alive, but I dreamed she had died. My father, who has been dead for nine years, was in the dream, but he was alive and I was talking to him. Dad and I were close. I said to my dad: 'Mom is dead. Can you take care of us, can you raise us alone?' He looked at me, hugged me, and said: 'Yes,

I can. I will do my best to raise you and your sister because I love you both very much.' When I woke up, I felt happy to see my dad, but horrified that my mother was dead."

Story Line: Inspired by love, someone confirms they can rise to the occasion.

Key Symbols:

MOTHER: Normally the main caregiver.

DEAD MOTHER: As a metaphor, the dead mother mirrors how incapable the dreamer feels as a single mother, as a feeling of loss of one's nurturing abilities.

TALKING WITH DEAD FATHER: A strong person dreamer trusted and was close to; a stand-in for dreamer's own strength.

ASKING DAD ABOUT RAISING CHILDREN ALONE: Dreamer is assessing her own strength and reconnecting to it.

THE WORDS "BECAUSE I LOVE YOU": Love of family inspired and motivated dreamer's father, qualities dreamer reconnects to during the conversation.

Analysis: When her boyfriend left without warning, Cindy parked herself at the edge of an emotional cliff. Feeling overwhelmed and with few skills, she did not feel she could be the mother she needed and wanted to be, to her children. The nightmare pointed the way. At her lowest, most vulnerable point, Cindy's dad was a gentle reminder of her own strength.

Cindy said: "That helped a lot."

Gentle Selfie, Example #4:
Selling My Soul to the Devil

The Dreamer: Corey grew up in a small town where he was raised according to strict fundamentalist Christian values of hard work, knowing your place, and family first. Though he tried his best, by age twenty-one Corey was floundering; he could not get a foothold into a career that made him happy. Battling depression and financial challenges, Corey prayed and prayed, but things were not falling into place.

The Nightmare Told in the Dreamer's Own Words:

"I had the same nightmare two nights in a row. The first night the dream began with snarling, barking dogs that charged into my bedroom. As the barking got louder and louder, I sat up in terror. All went quiet. The silence was broken by a demon who appeared in front of me and laughed. I asked why he was laughing. He said 'I am going to make your life a living hell.' I woke up in a panic.

"The second night, I saw myself in a new house. It was a mansion my family owned, though in real life we have little. The demon appeared again and put me in a car. As we drove, he pointed out my family's wealthy lifestyle and how the family now had everything anyone could want: cars, expensive watches, money. The devil said 'This is how your family could live if you were dead,' as if suggesting that I should die. Then the devil started to drive the car into a lake, to kill me. I screamed 'Why are you doing this?' He said 'Unless you sell me your soul, I am going to ruin your life.' I said 'What do I get in return?' He said 'What you always wanted—to be a millionaire.' As I agreed to sell my soul to the devil, he poked me in the chest and I woke up, feeling very, very scared. The dream felt so real, I wondered if I had actually sold my soul to the devil."

Story Line: Someone is willing to pay any price to achieve success.

Key Symbols:

ATTACKING DOGS AND LOUD BARKING: Feeling besieged by life's challenges; dreamer's fears.

LAUGHING DEMON: A contradiction; a nasty person who tries to look good.

THREAT TO MAKE LIFE A LIVING HELL: Dreamer's fear of what he will face in life.

MONEY AND WEALTH: What dreamer secretly wants.

Analysis: The nightmare addressed Corey's anxieties about earning a living and his conflict about wanting a good life. The verbal banter with the devil about wealth hinted that Corey thought money was evil, per his fundamentalist Christian upbringing, and had fears that earning a lot of money would send him to hell. Nevertheless, as the topic of their conversation, Corey wants to be rich and successful. As Corey tried to stifle a secret ambitious streak, the intense push–pull between emotions and his upbringing made him feel depressed. Corey wanted success but did not want to lose his soul.

Corey's fragile ego was afraid to claim a desire to be rich, so the nightmare gently converted his ambition into a forced deal with the devil. Hey—if it is forced on you, the deal can't be wrong. That was the mind game Corey played in the nightmare. To get straight with himself, Corey had to realize that both the rich and the poor face temptations; what counts is what you do with money, not how much you have.

The message was also a back-handed hint about the need to be realistic. There is no instant path to wealth, no deal to make with the devil or anyone else to earn a quick million. Much to the chagrin of some in an electronic age of instant everything, hard work and patience are still the price of admission to success and peace!

NIGHTMARE

Gentle Selfie, Example #5:
Husband Leaves, a Recurring Nightmare

The Dreamer: Carla was a seventy-four-year-old whose husband had died ten years earlier; Carla did not understand why she kept having the same dream about her husband, years after his death.

The Nightmare Told in the Dreamer's Own Words:

> "Every now and then I have the same nightmare where my dead husband is going back to his ex-wife. I had this dream when he was alive, too, and I still have it. The nightmare leaves me distressed, disconcerted, and afraid."

Story Line: Someone keeps re-experiencing being abandoned by a significant other.

Key Symbols:

ALWAYS LEAVING: Abandoned, feeling unloved; a loss.

EX-WIFE: In this dream, a symbol of an intruder from the past that interferes with the present.

Analysis: Carla had these nightmares when her husband was alive as well as after he died, which suggests that she never feel loved as she wanted—or needed—to be loved. The story hints that Carla never felt that her husband was completely committed to her. Whether it was true or merely how Carla felt, it was a gap in trust that left Carla feeling insecure and uncomfortable.

The nightmare highlighted Carla's feelings, saying "What would have made you feel loved when your husband was alive? What would it take, now, for you to feel loved? What is missing, now and then?" Because the nightmare went on for ten years after her husband was already dead, the nightmare was clearly about Carla, not her husband, as a repeated scene about feeling rejected. The story hinted that Carla felt low self-worth. As theory in modern popular psychology and as a counselor might point out, when someone does not love themselves, it's hard for them to feel loved by another.

Confronted by the nightmare, Carla needed to determine what had happened in childhood or during an early romantic experience that made her feel unloved and unworthy. Trauma early in life, such as the loss of a parent or abuse, can undermine feelings of self-confidence in later relationships. Whatever the source, the recurring nightmare invited Carla to name the pain and heal it.

Carla said: "Thank you so much!! That insight helped tremendously!!! I have been very insecure in relationships ever since my mom walked out on me when I was nine." *Take note:* Even at age seventy, thanks to a nightmare, Carla reconnected to a long-lost part of herself—an unidentified childhood pain. As a gentle shove, the nightmare substituted an image of "Carla's husband leaving" in place of "the departure of her mom," as a less threatening bookmark of Carla's pain. The childhood wound that had remained raw for a lifetime finally found healing.

Gentle Selfie, Example #6:
I Watch as My Wife Is Abused

The Dreamer: When he was thirty-seven, Richard's wife cheated on him. He and his wife reconciled and made the marriage work. A couple of years later, Richard was shocked by a nightmare.

Nightmare Told in the Dreamer's Own Words:

"My wife and I are at a friend's camper for the weekend, having a good time. Sometime during the day, my wife and I go to the bathroom. When we are done, there is a roller coaster nearby so we take a ride and had a good time. When the ride is finished, several guys nearby begin to brutally attack my wife. I am in anguish but can't do anything to help her."

Story Line: People have fun, find relief, enjoy ups and downs, yet in the end suffer.

Key Symbols:

CAMPER: A place where people relax and enjoy themselves.

BATHROOM: A metaphor for finding relief, letting go of what is toxic.

ROLLER COASTER: A visual for the ups and downs of life.

GETTING OFF THE ROLLER COASTER: Getting back to what is real; flags a turning point in the relationship, about getting real.

GROUP ATTACK: Intense anger and negativity directed at someone.

BYSTANDER WHO CANNOT HELP: An image of being helpless.

Analysis: At first, the saga logs the couple's emotional history. The couple finds ways to be together, to enjoy life, and to find relief. There are ups and downs, yet they have fun. Until . . . the crap unexpectedly hits the fan and there is pain and suffering on both sides.

Bonus Hint: When something in a dream surprises you, like this ending, flag the surprise as important. The end of a dream often shows the way forward: this ending depicts an unfair attack against someone who cannot defend themselves— the wife. But, as the element that surprises, it also begs the question: Why is the husband a helpless bystander?

Sometimes you have to reach beyond the obvious. You would expect a husband to battle the attackers instead of standing by, helpless. The fact that Richard makes no attempt to help his wife is a clue that the dream is *not* about his wife: it is about him, the husband. In a man's dream, a main female character such as a wife can be a symbol of the man's soft, vulnerable side. Take a second look at the ending through that lens: what was under attack was the husband's leftover feelings about the affair; as a gentle punch, the nightmare unmasked the cuckolded husband's secret pain. Two years after his wife's affair, Richard still felt emotionally beat up. In the nightmare, Richard was the husband standing by, helpless; he was also the woman—a metaphor of his vulnerable side—who was getting beat up. The message said: "Examine your true, secret feelings. You pretend that you worked things out, but the wound is still festering." As the nightmare pointed out, before the relationship could grow and deepen, Richard had to get honest about the lingering pain and what was likely hiding behind the pain—his unresolved anger. At every masquerade ball, the time arrives when the masks come off.

NIGHTMARE SELFIES AND PROJECTION

To keep you real and balanced, the psyche will on occasion point out a blind spot, disguised by actor stand-ins who portray your shortcomings. We tend to ignore our faults, and often we literally do not see them. When you're awake, you avoid the skeletons in your closet. When you're asleep, the blind spots become visible; and when warts and the like appear in a dream, it feels scary. Seeing someone else act ridiculous is fun, like watching a TV housewife toss water on a rival. When a boss makes a mistake and looks stupid, employees may get a kick out of it. But if you see that in a dream . . . well, you know the rest.

As a mind game we all play, projection is about hiding your gray areas from yourself. An uncle weaves in and out of traffic at high speed; he rants about bad drivers but does not see his own crappy road moves. A bully gets mad at others who push him around. A bad-tempered husband accuses his wife of doing things to upset him, yet is blind to his own rage. And the classic case is a preacher who is the loudest voice on the pulpit to condemn illicit sex . . . until others discover his secret sex life with prostitutes. That is projection: the bad that you notice in others tends to match your own blind spot, about yourself.

Think of projection in nightmares as a form of bait-and-switch that gets you past your resistant blind spots. Mesmerized, you watch a scene about a fellow employee who drinks too much and acts crazy. You admire a charmer who flirts, maybe even too much, with every woman he sees. Spoiler alert: Most dream characters are a hidden mirror of you.

Even if you put your hands over your ears and loudly say "La, la, la, la, la," a nightmare will find a way to deliver a critical message. One way is to overlay your shadows onto someone else.

Projection Nightmare, Example #1:
A Downward Spiral

The Dreamer: As a forty-two-year-old professional, Judith believed in helping others and did her best to live right. However, in a nightmare, she is shocked by what happens to a close middle-aged friend, Marlene, at a college library.

> Marlene is attending college and goes to the library to get a book. A young classmate gives Marlene a challenging look, then both try to grab the same book from a bookshelf. Judith, the dreamer, is horrified as her normally calm friend Marlene leaps between the bookshelves and pushes through a narrow opening with such force that the bookcase tilts and falls over. Books fall on the floor, making a mess. Feeling foolish and horrified, the dream friend, Marlene, knows she has to clean up the mess. Judith wakes up confused and horrified; she would never act that way, and neither would her friend Marlene.

Analysis: The story portrays someone who is easily baited into a silly competition that makes both people look ridiculous and ends badly. Judith scanned her life for parallels to the story. She was normally a poster child of a calm professional, like her friend Marlene, and did not see herself as competitive. Until . . . Judith realized that at recent meetings at work, a colleague had voiced strong opinions on topics that no one else cared about. Others let it pass, but Judith had been jumping in with passionate rebuttals that led to pointless arguments with the annoying colleague. Oops. Judith saw that *she* was the out-of-whack competitor who had a hidden need to win. Confronted with how silly the windmill attacks looked at meetings, there would be no more rebuttals. Judith decided to channel her feisty spirit into improving her skills, instead of petty arguments.

Projection Nightmare, Example #2:
Self-Inflicted Torture, Attacks, Killing

The Dreamer: As a sensitive sixteen-year-old, Andy experienced enormous pain as he watched his parents work through an acrimonious divorce.

> One night he had a blood-curdling nightmare: Andy watched a friend sit completely still, showing no emotion. Suddenly the friend picked up a hammer and sharp tools and began to gouge himself, creating extreme pain. What came next were horrible scenes of bombings, fire, killing, and the death of loved ones.

Analysis: In real life, Andy hid his pain about the divorce under a calm exterior and, when asked how he felt, said he was fine. Raised to be polite, Andy told others what they wanted to hear, not what was real.

The friend in the nightmare was a projection of Andy's anguish at the war his parents were waging; their animosity was mirrored in the bombs, killing, and destruction. Upset by the dream, Andrew talked with a family member who was a counselor, which gave him a chance to put words to his intense hidden feelings. Andy came to see that pushing his pain away could lead to depression—like the image of the friend sitting motionless. But at other times the pushed-away pain could erupt into an angry explosion at an insignificant annoyance, which had happened to Andy. Neither repressing the hurt nor letting it explode was helpful. Though it would take time to sort out his feelings, the nightmare and a helpful relative put Andy on the road to healing.

Projection Nightmare, Example #3:
Ellen's Appearance Struggles

Not all nightmares have blood and gore; some simply shove an uncomfortable clash in your face.

The Dreamer: As a lively and pretty twenty-seven-year-old, Ellen was obsessed with her weight and her looks. She also loved sweets and fine dining, opposites that led to constant ups and downs in her appearance, weight, and self-confidence. A series of nightmares logged Ellen's inner struggle.

Breaking the Law

In one nightmare, Ellen saw two women in an apartment who deliberately lock the front door because they are about to smoke pot in a city where marijuana was illegal. A journalist gets wind of what they are doing and knocks on the door. The ladies ignore the knocks and continue doing what they want. Ellen woke up. She felt unnerved; breaking the law was not in her wheelhouse.

Analysis: The pot-smoking women were a projection of Ellen's tendency to binge on sweets, which Ellen knew was not right; yet she justified her binges as a stress-buster. Ellen understood that the dream was about her willful behavior and acknowledged her blind spot, sort of. She admitted that the sweet binges were not good for her, but she was not ready to rein in her sweet tooth. Dreams point out what is true, but only dreamers can decide what they do about it, or when.

Claiming the Coveted Prize

In another nightmare, Ellen sees a chubby young woman who has won a free pass to a spa, a prize that is worth thousands of dollars and would transform her body. It is a deal no one would refuse. But the chubby young prize-winner is wishy-washy about claiming her prize. She vacillates a dozen times, then finally decides to take the spa and fitness package, and commits to doing it. Ellen wakes up in a cold sweat, knowing that *she* was the wishy-washy prize-winner.

Analysis: A few days earlier, Ellen had read a book about getting healthy; she knew that if she followed the book's advice, she could achieve the balance she longed for in health, sweets, and appearance. Ellen sank back onto her pillow, owning her dark side—an addiction to sweets. Yes, sweets were okay in moderation, but going overboard regularly, as she did . . . not so much. Ellen desperately wanted to make a fresh start, but ice cream and chocolate still beckoned. Sound familiar? Did Ellen adopt a healthy spa way of life of fresh fruits, veggies, and exercise after this nightmare? You guessed it: not yet. Nevertheless, like yeast in a dough, the nightmare confrontations began to have an effect. Ellen began to nibble less on junk food and slowly began to drop a few unwanted pounds.

A Painful Turning Point—Jane Fonda Visits

Jane Fonda was one of Ellen's favorite role models as someone who came to terms with her body and learned to age with grace and good health. In Ellen's final nightmare, Jane Fonda was giving a radio interview about a seminar, and mentioned that she would bring cookies to the seminar. The lady radio host brashly tells Jane Fonda that she does not eat cookies because she has to lose weight. Jane Fonda does not buy it; she guesses that the host secretly eats any dessert set in front of her and publicly exposes the host's secret. The public announcement by Jane Fonda that the host eats a lot of sweets, which is true, fills the host with shame.

Analysis: Ellen wakes up feeling horrible, as if *she* is the radio host who has been exposed by Jane Fonda. And she was. Ellen felt devastated. The nightmare rebuke from her cherished role model, who was also a projection of her best self, stung beyond words. It was time to get down to business and handle her runaway sweet tooth.

Months later, a final dream logged Ellen's continuing saga.

Damn, Girl, You Look Good

Ellen is at a conference and crosses paths with a former colleague, an attractive friend who also has struggled with weight. The friend now looks like a gorgeous fashion model. Ellen says "Wow, you've lost a lot of weight: you look great!" The friend appreciates the compliment and shares how hard she has worked to achieve it. As Ellen woke up, she felt inspired by the friend's success: the dream was a gentle nudge to get herself to the finish line of her new health program.

Analysis: As a positive projection, the dream colleague cemented Ellen's commitment. With a new zip in her step, Ellen knew she could attain a slender body within a healthy lifestyle that included sweet treats, in balance.

Projection Nightmare, Example #4:
The Highway Madman

The Dreamer: As a twenty-five-year-old ex-soldier and unemployed army engineer from the Midwest, Daniel had a lot of pent-up anger. Unable to find work in his hometown, his rage grew; he felt the government had left him and his family in the lurch. No stranger to bad dreams during this frustrating time, Daniel had a nightmare that disturbed him for days.

The Nightmare Told in the Dreamer's Own Words:

"As I drive home from Cleveland, in my car mirror I notice a tall blue flame in the sky. I stop to see what it is. Just then, there is a large explosion. A car is on fire and catapults past me; those inside are trapped. A crowd gathers. Someone says that a crazed man who had highly unstable chemicals caused a huge catastrophe on the highway, and an ungodly number of people are dead or dying. Military police are rounding up suspects and doing mercy killings on those who cannot be saved. I decide to leave as quickly as possible; I call my mother and fiancée to say that I am on my way home. As I hang up, I see a military roadblock ahead. I try to force my way through; it does not work. As my car comes to a stop, a large, angry soldier marches up to my window, reaches in through broken glass, and begins to pull me through. I reach for the pistol that I hide under my driver's seat, point the muzzle at him, and pull the trigger. I wake up terrified, feeling angry and helpless."

Story Line: Someone on their way to where they belong encounters horrible effects created by someone who is out of control; as they seek a way out, they are threatened, yet survive.

Key Symbols:

BLUE FLAME: An image of a pilot light, something that ignites. As the first metaphor in the dream, it suggests the dreamer's intense, ignited feelings as the issue.

EXPLOSION: Metaphor for dreamer's explosive feelings.

CRAZED MAN: A projection of how the dreamer feels because his life is not working.

HIGHLY UNSTABLE CHEMICALS: Emotions veering out of control. They could cause harm.

PEOPLE DEAD OR DYING: The negative changes the dreamer sees around him.

MILITARY POLICE: A projection of dreamer's lawful and law-abiding side. Rounding up suspects hints that the dreamer wants to get back on track.

MERCY KILLINGS: Points to the dreamer's sensitive side; he hates to see people suffer.

CRAZED SOLDIER WHO ATTACKS DREAMER: Projection of dreamer's anger that can hurt himself and others.

Analysis: The nightmare shows the clash between Daniel's cool, educated engineer's mind and the ticking time bomb of his explosive feelings. His life had hit a brick wall. In the nightmare, Daniel faces his rage—a violent, uncontrollable anger that makes him feel he is under attack. The cool-headed part of Daniel knew he had to rein in his anger. As the nightmare ends, he fights the crazed soldier, who is a projection of his own mindless rage. As Daniel kills the soldier, he takes back his power and takes control of his emotions, before they can do any damage.

Daniel woke up feeling helpless and terrified. Seeing himself go crazy in the nightmare scared Daniel into landing on his feet. Daniel lived to fight another day; sometimes that is the best you can do. Some inner challenges can be hard to pinpoint while awake but are mirrored in dreams. Meeting a negative projection of yourself can open up a safety valve.

Projection Nightmare, Example #5:
A Dying Pigeon

The Dreamer: Forty-one-year-old Carrie had broken up with her boyfriend and, although he was on her mind a lot, she was dating others and moving on.

The Nightmare Told in the Dreamer's Own Words:
"My ex-boyfriend gives me a pigeon, which I keep in a cage in my garage. He asks about the pigeon. I realize I've completely forgotten about it and the bird has had no food or water for days. I panic, worried that the pigeon is dead, but when I get to the garage it is still alive. I reach into the cage to take out the food and water bowls. The pigeon tries to escape and gets out, but after for a minute of chasing it around the garage I catch it. I hold the pigeon in my hand. I feel both great love and pity for the creature, and I feel bad about putting it back in the cage. In a deep, intense moment, I realize the pigeon should not have to live in a cage, yet I feel compelled to take care of it and protect it. I reluctantly put the bird back into the cage and bring it food and water. I wake up feeling tremendous love for the bird and an urge to nurture and protect it. At the same time, there is pain, sadness, and regret, about having to put it back in the cage."

Story Line: Someone struggles with a decision about freedom versus safety with limitations.

Key Symbols:

PIGEON: A bird that always returns home, an issue about home. A projection of dreamer's thoughts about a relationship.

FOOD AND WATER: What we need to survive; metaphor for love and a relationship.

BIRD ESCAPES AND IS CAUGHT: Beginnings and endings; freedom versus safety.

CAGE: What limits yet also protects.

KEEPING BIRD IN THE GARAGE: Keeping something at arm's length, not quite owning it, not letting something fully into one's heart or space.

Analysis: As a gift from her ex, the "home-ing" pigeon hinted that Carrie's relationship with her ex awakened Carrie's desire for a home and family. At the same time, the pigeon is a projection of Carrie's dilemma: when the relationship ended, Carrie felt free, yet her need for love felt starved and neglected. The pigeon's escape points to issues about freedom versus closeness. On the one hand, Carrie loved the freedom of being single without the constraints a relationship brings; on the other hand, she missed the safety, caring, and closeness of a relationship. The nightmare confronted Carrie with her conflicted feelings: a desire for freedom that was at odds with security and closeness needs.

Thinking it through, Carrie concluded that her opposing needs did not have to be an either/or choice. Art expressed her free spirit, and she loved to travel. Traveling to art seminars could fulfill Carrie's need for freedom, an interest that could be anchored by a home and a relationship. When Carrie put the pigeon back into the cage in the dream, the act harmonized her conflicted feelings; she accepted that a loving relationship was worth a few limitations. The nightmare was "an emotional exercise class" that allowed Carrie to work out her conflict. Despite a touch of buyer's remorse as she woke up, Carrie had decided that a secure relationship was her best track.

Carrie said: "Thank you so much! Your interpretation is spot on. The ex-BF had commitment issues which led to the breakup; afterward, I saw I had commitment issues too. You are right, I am the pigeon. It makes so much sense about why I was so conflicted about putting the bird back in the cage, yet decided it felt right. I thought the dream was about learning to let go, but it was so much more!"

NIGHTMARE

Projection Nightmare, Example #6:
Ghost Girl

The Dreamer: Iris was a twenty-four-year-old single mom of two children recovering from a recent marriage breakup. Iris had a lot of anxiety about being alone and began having nightmares about a ghost attack.

The Nightmare Told in the Dreamer's Own Words:

"I had this dream a few times. I am in bed in my own house. A young girl appears; she is a ghost. The girl is about ten years old, with blond curly hair. I don't recognize her. I feel I have to block the ghost girl and prevent her from attacking me. I wake up in a panic. It feels as if the ghost girl is still in my house. I feel scared. In one dream she attacked me, pinned me to the ceiling, then threw me around. These dreams terrify me."

Story Line: Someone struggles with a being from the past that threatens and controls them.

Key Symbols:

> GHOST: Something from the past.
>
> TEN-YEAR-OLD GIRL: Normally, someone who is vulnerable and innocent.
>
> BLOCKING THE GHOST: Fighting and engaging with something from the past.
>
> ATTACKED: Feeling vulnerable, under siege.
>
> HELD UP TO THE CEILING: Raised and pinned down; being controlled, control issues.
>
> THROWN AROUND BY A GHOST: Brings to mind scary movies about being possessed; may hint that dreamer feels controlled or out of control.

Analysis: The frequent nightmares mirrored how Iris felt: vulnerable and afraid. The ghost was a projection of her fears. Iris had been thrown into a new life as a single mother, a life for which she felt emotionally unprepared; she was not coping. The nightmare appears to confront Iris about her dark, petrified state of mind. Or does it?

Bonus Hint: Sometimes you have to peek beyond the obvious and look for a deeper message. The ghost was a projection of the dreamer's fears; but why is the ghost a ten-year-old girl? Whatever surprises or does not fit can be a pivotal image. In scary movies about being possessed, it is always a young girl who is thrown around by demons. But . . . this ten-year-old ghost is a powerhouse of strength who lifts Iris up and throws her to the ceiling. The young girl's strength is a major feature, and the key to what the young ghost is all about. Ghost girl is a projection of Iris—as Iris once was in her youth: strong, powerful, and someone who could stand up for herself. Ghost girl wants to "re-possess" the dreamer so that Iris can reclaim her strength. As a projection of the stronger part of herself—as well as her fears—ghost girl was on a mission to shake Iris up, take over, and reconnect Iris to her empowered self. Iris did get a grip on her fears; the sassy young girl was back.

NIGHTMARE

Projection Nightmare, Example #7:
Groping a Mannequin in the Dark

The Dreamer: Annabel was an exhausted twenty-five-year-old who was completing her last year of graduate school. Eager to begin her life as a professional, in her last semester Annabel was just going through the motions. She felt depressed, alone, and unsupported. As a further slap in the face, a nightmare rattled Annabel's normally calm composure.

The Nightmare Told in the Dreamer's Own Words:

"I am at an outdoor concert. Suddenly everyone disappears and there is total darkness. I could not see anything, but I felt someone around me and thought it was my best friend. I said 'Emma, is that you,' but she never answered. It was so dark. I pull my phone out and call her, saying 'Emma, are you messing with me?' She said: 'No, I'm at home, studying.' I said: 'No, you're not, you're here in front of me, but I can't see you.' Before Emma could answer, I walked up to whatever is in front of me and grabbed its face. Instead of flesh, my hand feels clay, like a dummy made of a rubbery substance. I can feel its nose, eyes, and a cheek, beneath a gooey skin. I freak out; it is not Emma.

Suddenly I feel a live presence behind me; it moves, scratches my back, and rips the skin of my back open, into a huge gash, making me bleed. I am petrified and in pain, I can't see what scratched me or why. In the dream I wake up, but I am still asleep, watching myself wake up from a scary dream. Seconds later, I actually wake up."

Story Line: Someone assumes that an unseen presence is friendly, but discovers it is something fake that hurts them.

Key Symbols:

OUTDOOR CONCERT: What is out in the open; what cannot hide.

CROWDS DISAPPEAR: A metaphor for facing oneself; nothing matters except you.

DARKNESS, IN THE DARK: Being out of touch with oneself.

A MANNEQUIN, DUMMY: A lifeless being, an empty shell; mirrors how dreamer feels.

SCRATCH AND SKIN RIPPED OPEN: Metaphor of pain that suddenly opens up dreamer's feelings.

A GASH, A DEEP WOUND: Image of pain, projection of dreamer's pushed-away emotions.

BEING AWAKE IN A DREAM: When you are dreaming and realize you are dreaming, that is called lucid dreaming. Sometimes the sleeping and awake minds cross paths; it can be a moment of intense awareness that creates a leap in understanding.

Analysis: With a dark night as a metaphor of feeling lost, emotionally, the dreamer had to confront her shadows. The crowds were gone; the public mask she wore no longer counted. Feeling out of touch with herself, Annabel reached out to a friend. Like Annabel, the friend is at home and hard at work; the over-achiever friend is a projection of Annabel's ambitious side. To pursue her career goals, Annabel had pushed emotions aside so completely that she now lived only in her head. In the nightmare, she confronts her repressed feelings. The scary mannequin is a projection of the lifeless emotional shell Annabel has become: in her daily life, Annabel looks human and plays her part; but inside, she feels nothing. The scary creature who wounds her makes Annabel feel something—a pain that restores her connection to her emotions.

Scratching someone's back is a play on the expression "You scratch my back and I will scratch yours," as a pact between colleagues to help each other. As a projection of Annabel's repressed emotions, the unknown scratcher, as a projection of Annabel's unconscious self, had agreed to hold her feelings in the background for her until she needed them. But Annabel went too far—she disowned *all* her emotions and cut herself off from herself, including her ability to enjoy life. The mannequin attacker said "Feel the pain; this is you." The mannequin was a visual pun about reopening her feelings.

The lucid moment at the end of Annabel's nightmare was a moment when she became aware of her emotional state; it was a psychological leap in understanding, and a healing. As a lucid push, the nightmare said "Look, you can feel again, even if it is pain; wake up and be whole." Once Annabel gave herself permission to feel again—to play and let loose as well as work—she no longer felt like a robot. Sometimes meeting your dark side is like heart surgery: it re-opens a clogged path and restores the flow of harmony, peace, and joy.

NIGHTMARE SELFIES AND MORALITY

Some challenges make you grapple with what you believe and how you apply those beliefs. Edgar Cayce was a famous healer and clairvoyant in Virginia Beach; known as the Sleeping Prophet, he could access information from a heavenly perch. After he entered a semi-trance, Cayce answered many questions about health and the meaning of life; as he spoke, someone took notes. In one reading, Cayce defined sleep as the soul taking stock of what it had done the day before, suggesting that, during sleep, you evaluate your life against your ideals and standards. However, Cayce continued, such dreams are not there to condemn: they are an expression of inner conflict. That was true for Stanley, who had a nightmare about a giant crane that came crashing down on the roof of his house. The horrifying scene paralleled the damage Stanley could do if he continued his secret love affair. The nightmare said "You believe in marriage, and by breaking your vows you risk losing home and family. Is that what you want?" A morality nightmare states the issue and its consequences, but only the dreamer can choose what to do next.

Whether it is a scene from Shakespeare's *Hamlet* or a modern television or movie drama, the ongoing battle between the good and the not-so-good is the stuff of life, as played out in these examples.

NIGHTMARE

Morality Nightmare, Example #1:
Betrayed

The Dreamer: Sophia was a thirty-two-year-old housewife who was raising five children. When her husband cheated on her, Sophia was shocked and dismayed. As she tiptoed through her wounded feelings, a dozen recurring nightmares flagged moral dilemma: should she stay, or leave?

In one nightmare, Sophia sees herself shaking violently, yet unable to cry; she just sits alone in the dark, devastated, unable to see or hear anything. Then she wakes up in terror. In one variation, Sophia sees her husband with his girlfriend; it infuriates Sophia. Another dream offers a glimmer of hope, as Sophia and her husband cordially talk about Paris, a vacation they had always wished to take. Should she forgive him? Could she forgive him? Nightmares mirrored her dilemma, but only Sophia could choose.

The Dreamer: Facing a similar situation at age thirty-seven, Rachel's husband had an affair and got the other woman pregnant. "Betrayed" did not adequately describe Rachel's anguish.

In one nightmare, she watches her husband get shot with a shotgun; it mirrored her rage. As he dies in the dream, her husband's final words are "I love my wife."

Analysis: Rachel believed in love, marriage, and fidelity, a moral code her husband's betrayal severely tested, especially with another woman's child as a forever reminder of his infidelity. Challenging Rachel's ideals, the nightmare asks: If he died tomorrow and still loves you, how would you feel? Would you forgive him?

Both wives faced the same moral dilemma: both had nightmares that evoked critical questions related to their standards and ideals. Each had to make decisions that would dramatically affect their lives. However . . . their nightmares did not appear to offer hints about what path to take. How come?

WHAT IF THERE'S NO CLEAR SOLUTION TO A PROBLEM?

There are several reasons a dream may not offer an answer for a dilemma you face.

* *Mirror.* Sometimes what you need is a mirror of what you feel and think, especially at the beginning of a dilemma. You may need to feel your way through and assess your feelings before you make a decision. Dreams are a great mirror for feelings.

* *Not Ready for Answers.* Have you ever heard someone rant and rave about what happened to them? Highly emotional, they can't stop talking about the incident, repeating the same things over and over. They are in reaction mode, reacting to some event. If you get a word in edgewise, they don't seem to hear a thing you say and keep ranting. And even though you want to help, eventually you realize the person is not ready to hear what you have to say. Intense turmoil and confusion can leave someone deaf to advice—including advice from their own soul and psyche, as dream hints. When their emotional wheels eventually stop spinning, dreams will again relay suggestions and solutions.

* *Dream Hints and Bias.* Sometimes there is only one answer you want to hear. For the two wives described on pages 70–71 who were cheated on, when they first hear about their husband's betrayal, one may want her husband back at any cost; the other wife may want a divorce. Both start with a bias, and even though either option works, dreams can hint which path might work out best, including when, and how. However, the dreamer must be able to set aside their initial bias. Whether in dreams or in life, you have to be ready to hear the truth.

* *Six of One and a Half Dozen of the Other.* Sometimes a decision, such as whether to leave or to remain in a relationship—is simply a choice. Each option has positives and negatives; each brings challenges, joys, and possibilities. When the matter is simply a choice, assessing your ideals, goals, and beliefs can be the best deciding factor.

Bonus Hint About Real or Fake Images: Look out for dreams that ask you to evaluate what is true or false—such as whether a jewel is real or fake, or if a dog is purebred or a Heinz variety. Such "real or fake" dreams ask you to assess your goals, beliefs, and standards, as in: Before you make a decision on this issue, evaluate what is true or false for you about the topic. Otherwise, your choice will not feel authentic or come out right.

Morality Nightmare, Example #2:
To Be or Not To Be . . . Together

The Dreamer: Thirty-three-year-old Lydia had a two-year-old toddler. She also had an in-law problem that interfered with her marriage and became so challenging that she and her husband separated for a few weeks. It was not clear to Lydia or to her husband whether the separation would be temporary or permanent.

> In a nightmare, Lydia saw herself and her husband rush to the hospital after a car crash; at the hospital, she sees her husband drawn to a younger woman. Lydia does not condemn his roving eye; he appreciates her understanding, and they reconcile. Lydia woke up in a cold sweat, terrified. If she stayed away, she wondered, would she lose her husband to a younger woman?

Analysis: As a morality tale, the nightmare spoke of a shady momentary lapse—the husband merely looked; he did not act. The dream also showed how a good attitude brought reconciliation; that was a hint for Lydia. Whatever grievances she had with her in-laws, understanding and forgiveness could heal the situation.

In a second nightmare, Lydia was horrified to see herself as a bride without a groom; nevertheless, she gets married with everybody's blessing. To whom was she making a commitment? Sometimes in a woman's dream, a man can represent her own strengths; in this case, the absent groom was a metaphor of Lydia's disconnecting from her strengths because of her recent troubles. The one-sided marriage, happening with everyone's blessing, portrayed Lydia reconnecting to her strengths. This nightmare hinted that by staying strong, she could keep her marriage and her life on track, no matter what; the next move was Lydia's. She chose wisely and went back into the marriage with understanding and a good attitude.

Morality Nightmare, Example #3:
An Attack on Helpless Creatures

The Dreamer: At the age of twenty-seven, Fred was in love. His new relationship felt amazing—until a scary nightmare confused the heck out of Fred.

> In the dream, Fred and his girlfriend are out to dinner with friends. As they sit at the table, several ghosts keep trying to kill two small, defenseless dogs who are nearby. No one seems to care, except Fred. As he woke up, the attempted murder of the helpless pups bothered Fred beyond words. He loved dogs and would never hurt anyone, so why the nightmare?

Analysis: On the surface, the new relationship was great; Fred and his girlfriend were in love, and they were about to move in together. Except. . . . His psyche knew a secret that Fred and his girlfriend had not told anyone. His girlfriend was married and was about to leave her husband and move in with Fred; and, in secret, his new girlfriend planned to take her young son away from his father, without forewarning her husband.

Oops. To his credit, the plan did not sit well with Fred's conscience. The nightmare whispered, "That is a nasty plan, akin to watching someone attack a helpless puppy; it will destroy your peace of mind." Nudged by the nightmare, Fred knew that he and his girlfriend had to confront the husband. Even if his girlfriend's marriage was over, leaving the husband on the sly was not honorable. As a morality tale, Fred's nightmare reminded him that he valued integrity; it inspired Fred to do right by the ex-husband and child. Score ten points for morality nightmares.

HERBERT COLE 19

CHAPTER FIVE

Nightmares as True, Literal Warnings

Like a blind man's walking stick that reveals a bump in the road, a nightmare can warn you, though you may still have to decipher what the challenge is and how to deal with it. Like a yellow traffic signal, a warning nightmare screams, "Put the brakes on, stay alert, assess what you see as you go forward." A nightmare about a physical symptom can inspire you to check out a health issue. A nightmare about a car crash can suggest a need to stop fighting to avoid the crash of a divorce. There are limits to what a warning dream can do. Sometimes a warning helps to avert the worst. At other times, all a nightmare warning can do is prepare you for the shock of the inevitable.

LITERAL DREAM WARNINGS

Dreams often exaggerate to get your attention, so an extreme nightmare is not an automatic life-or-death warning, though in rare cases, it can be a literal ESP warning.

Features of a Literal Dream Warning

The following checklist of features can help you determine whether a nightmare is a literal warning or a standard, metaphoric, scary exaggeration.

* *Repetition.* You have the nightmare several times, with similar details.

* *Intensity.* The nightmare is vivid and intense.

* *Actual Details.* Literal, true-to-life details such as people and locations you recognize.

* *Appropriate Reactions.* Reactions in the nightmare and when you wake up are appropriate to the story, and how characters behave in the story, is logical.

If all these factors are present, the nightmare could be a literal warning. Even so, hold off on the normal tendency to jump to conclusions. Try the following suggestions to assess the nightmare and its message.

Analyze the Nightmare As If It's a Regular Dream

Before deciding the nightmare is a warning, use the Five Step Dream Analysis Method outlined in Chapter Two to evaluate the story as if it's a normal dream. Take a step back. Though you may feel frightened, emotions do not necessarily flag a literal warning. See what turns up as a story line and how the story line may relate to a life issue. Once you translate even a terrifying nightmare into its generalities, the dream often fits a life situation or highlights a fear. After you analyze the dream using the five step method and still feel unsure, do the following:

* *Record the Nightmare.* Jot the nightmare down, complete with details. Add notes about issues, emotions, and concerns going on in your life.

* *Link to Life.* Track story parallels to your life.

* *Similar Dreams.* Keep an eye out for dreams with similar story lines.

Ask for a New Dream

To be absolutely sure if a nightmare is a literal warning, there is one more step you can try out. You carry on a daily dialogue with your psyche as a silent conversation of thoughts and feelings. Newsflash: The psyche—the "manager" part of you—notes your questions and concerns and answers them as dream messages! So to the surprise of many—you can intentionally plug in to that dialogue and ask your psyche a direct question! When confronted by a terrifying nightmare, ask your psyche to clarify the message in a new, more direct way. Keep your question simple. You can say: Was the nightmare a literal warning, yes or no? Or: Is the nightmare about issue x, yes or no? Ask questions on different nights and wait for a response before going on to the next question; it can take several nights to get an answer to. Also note that the psyche answers a question exactly as you ask it; so jot your question down, to remember how you phrased it.

See what dreams you get in response and evaluate the overall effect of the story. Scenes of sunshine and blue skies tend to accompany a positive response. Dark, gloomy roads and shadowy figures appear alongside negative indicators.

Try such a dialogue with your psyche and see what happens.

Bonus Hint: You can ask your psyche for a marker that tells you the dream is an answer to your question. For example, a color can be a dream marker: You can color-code "yes" and "no" options with a color of your choice. That works for many to clarify responses that come from a dialogue with the psyche.

DEATH AS A LITERAL WARNING

As the following four examples show, the Grim Reaper and other metaphors about death can flag a wide array of literal nightmare warnings.

NIGHTMARE

Literal Warning, Example #1:
A Motorcycle Disaster

The Dreamer: Thirty-two-year-old Ryan had a coworker, John, who was good-hearted, yet also a headstrong loner.

> In a blood-curdling nightmare, Ryan saw John racing his motorcycle up a steep city hill. As John rounds a sharp corner at breakneck speed, his motorcycle jumps out of control and begins to slide backward. Ryan watches in horror as John is thrown from his motorcycle and, in a gruesome death scene, sees John's body smashed, his limbs flying in all directions.

Analysis: Waking up extremely disturbed, Ryan had no clue what the nightmare meant. The scene was intense, showed an actual coworker on his bike, and took place on an actual street close to where they worked. When Ryan arrived at his desk that morning, he was relieved to see John close by, acting like his normal self. Ryan shrugged off the gruesome dream as indigestion from a late-night pizza. Until . . . months later. The terrifying dream made sense when John, depressed from a recent divorce, deliberately crashed his motorcycle and died, ending a secret battle with unbearable hurt. Though what others feel or do is not in our hands, Ryan's heart seared with pain. Would it have made a difference if he had spent time with John at lunch once in a while? Would conversations beyond the superficial have helped? There were no answers. All was now in God's hands.

NIGHTMARE

Literal Warning, Example #2:
A Sudden Attack

The Dreamer: In a nightmare, forty-two-year-old Daphne has a conversation with her close friend Abbey, a conversation that becomes more and more distressing.

> As the scene opens, Abbey shares that someone is trying to harm her by throwing stones. Yet Abbey shrugs off the threats and the attacks as inconsequential. As they keep talking, Daphne watches the thug approach Abbey, closer and closer, and with each step the thug wields a more dangerous weapon to use against Abbey. Abbey keeps retreating and shrugging off the threat. Finally there is no place left for Abbey to retreat except onto a narrow balcony. Daphne watches in horror as the assailant begins a life-and-death attack against Abbey; only one of them will come out alive. Frightened, Abbey finally takes the threat seriously and begins to shield herself, but it is too late; the attacker leaps onto the balcony and kills Abbey as Daphne wakes up with a horrified shudder.

Analysis: As a story line, the dream said "Someone ignores what is menacing, until they can no longer survive the threat." Such a story did not resonate for Daphne: she always met challenges head-on. Except. . . . Daphne had a cousin who was like a sister, a cousin dealing with a serious bout of cancer. The cousin had stopped responding to treatments, yet shrugged off dire predictions of having only a few months to live. Daphne felt calm; her cousin was a fighter. Still, within days, the cousin took a turn for the worse and passed away. Grieving, Daphne understood her nightmare, whose message said "Your dear cousin's illness reached a point where there was no way out." Daphne accepted the loss; her cousin had faced each day with courage. She felt strangely comforted by a nightmare story that held a distant echo of an intricate, mysterious, Divine plan—about life and death.

`NIGHTMARE`

Literal Warning, Example #3:
Weddings and Dead Relatives

The Dreamer: Imani was a South African woman who was interested in dreams. When her ninety-three-year-old grandmother had three scary dreams in a week, both Imani and her grandmother were disturbed. The scenes were not blood-curdling, yet her grandmother woke up distressed and frightened.

> In the first nightmare, her grandmother is about to get married in a pink dress, but nothing feels right. She does not know who she is marrying and does not recognize anyone at the church. In the second nightmare, the grandmother is again getting married. This time, she wears a white dress and is about to marry the ex-husband she divorced ten years earlier. The thought of marrying the ex again was extremely disturbing. In a third nightmare, the family digs up the coffin of the grandmother's

dead sister. The dead sister looks beautiful, exactly as she had before she died five years earlier. Though Imani's grandmother is happy to see her sister, the scene feels strange and scary.

Analysis: As a metaphor, marriage signals a future long-term commitment; however, these strange marriage scenes connected the grandmother to her past. The grandmother's health was ailing. Take note: glimpses of those who have passed on, in the dreams of those who are elderly or ill, can be a hint that they are preparing for the afterlife. In these dreams, scenes of a new commitment, strangers who feel uncomfortable, and appearances by those who died, were hints that, at a soul level, Imani's grandmother was getting ready to join her sister and her ex-husband in the hereafter. Whether the prospect of dying feels grim and scary or draws someone forward as a peaceful transition, in the end, death beckons one and all.

NIGHTMARE

Literal Warning, Example #4:
The Death of a Beloved Pet

The Dreamer: Dreams can bring unusual messages; one unusual dream communication relates to pets. Many report dreams about pets they love, living and dead, and describe nightmares about a pet's death, as in this example. Mia loved all creatures great and small. She often rescued neighborhood cats, like the pale orange kitty that wandered regularly down her street, singing a loud meow as it walked. When Mia saw the cat crouched in a corner during a major storm, she knew it was homeless and began to befriend the wandering stranger. Though initially skittish, the cat responded to tins of tuna and Mia's gentle touch; from its loving nature, Mia surmised it had once been someone's beloved pet. Within a few months, Tigger cherished moments of lap time with Mia in a warm, safe home. When playing outdoors, Tigger still sang his loud signature meow. One day Mia put two and two together. Her new pet never responded to her voice when she called, as other kitties did. And then there were the loud meows. Oops, Tigger was a special-needs kitty: he was deaf.

> Several years into their companionship, Mia was shocked by a nightmare in which Tigger runs from a kind, chubby friend of hers. To her surprise, the friend suddenly becomes gaunt and turns into the Grim Reaper, chasing Tigger with a crazed glint in his eye. In the dream, Mia rescues her pet; yet when she awoke, Mia felt greatly disturbed.

She pushed the images aside and forgot about the nightmare. It was only a dream. Until. . . . months later, Mia returned from a weekend trip; as always, Tigger was overjoyed to see her, yet he looked a bit thin. Within hours, Mia knew Tigger was in the throes of death and summoned a vet to make an immediate house call, to ensure a painless ending. But her sweet pet could not wait. Ending his life as a beloved kitty, Tigger took his last breath, soothed by Mia's gentle touch.

NIGHTMARE WARNINGS THAT ARE IMPORTANT, BUT NOT LITERAL

Most nightmares are not a literal warning but are important, anyway. Like all scary dreams, non-literal nightmare warnings use frightening metaphors to highlight a matter that needs your attention. Riding an elevator that crashes can speak of mood swings or feelings that are out of balance. Losing your teeth can be a warning to see a dentist, or a metaphor about careless words that hurt loved ones. An airplane crash can symbolize an idea that does not work or take off, as a warning about a project heading for failure. The following examples illustrate metaphoric warnings about all types of life issues.

Non-Literal Warning, Example #1:
Lucy's Story: Car Troubles

The Dreamer: Dreams can flag ongoing concerns, as they did for Lucy. At age fifty, Lucy was not a nervous driver yet had mild anxiety about having a car accident. As an unconscious cue, Lucy's fear became an automatic, unconscious request to her psyche to give her a dream heads-up in case car trouble was brewing. Like a good friend, her psyche came through with regular dream warnings about flat tires, faulty brakes, and an engine on the verge of a breakdown.

The Empty Road

One nightmare showed Lucy losing control of her steering because of a flat tire. Lucy often drove through a construction zone, so the possibility seemed real. Feeling smug about the dream warning, Lucy checked with her mechanic, who, after a quick eyeball of her tires, said all was well. Lucy dismissed the nightmare and forgot about it.

Though she rarely worked past five o'clock, a few days later, Lucy worked till about seven p.m. to finish a report, then headed for the highway. Minutes later, her car wobbled, lost speed, and—oops, Lucy knew she had a flat tire. The car veered into an adjacent lane a couple of times but rush hour was over, so no other cars were nearby: Lucy's nightmare caught what the mechanic had missed. Whether due to an unconscious cue or the help of a guardian angel, Lucy got home safely, with no danger to others.

A Break-In

For several years, Lucy lived in a secluded neighborhood in the middle of a forest. The area was so safe that for years she did not lock her car doors and she jokingly told herself, "If my car is ever in danger, a dream will warn me." A few years later, neighbors renovated their home, bringing dozens of out-of-town workers to their quiet cul-de-sac. Lucy never gave the next-door construction a second thought—until a loud voice in a dream said "Lock your car doors!" Thanks to previous warnings that panned out, Lucy did just that.

Nightmares and the Motivation of Others

Dreams can warn you about others' motives, thoughts, and feelings, and about what is happening in a relationship:

NIGHTMARE

Non-Literal Warning, Example #2:
I Cheat Regularly

The Dreamer: Still single at age twenty-eight, Francesca did not see herself as desperate; however, with a lot of married friends, she was eager to be in a relationship. After meeting a handsome man who had a good career, she threw herself into the relationship and did not mind being at his beck and call, most of which were booty calls. All seemed well, until Francesca was disturbed by a series of nightmares, like this one.

The Nightmare Told in the Dreamer's Own Words:

"My boyfriend and I are in a group; he pays no attention to me and hangs out with others. At some point he has a problem; and instead of coming to me, my boyfriend visits a lady down the street. I suspect something is going on between them, but don't know for sure. I am disappointed, but I overlook what might be going on because I really want the relationship to work. My boyfriend's best friend comes to me and says 'He loves them and leaves them.' He mentions that I am one of many. I hear the best friend's words but don't want to believe them." Francesca woke up angry and disturbed.

Analysis: The message was specific, telling her that her boyfriend was unfaithful and would never commit. Yet as Francesca told herself in the dream, she wanted the relationship to work, so she shrugged off the dream. Hope, as an emotion, can be as blinding as fear. After several similar nightmares and reality checks about her boyfriend's wandering eye, Francesca finally accepted the nightmare warnings and moved on.

Bonus Hint: When words are spoken in a dream, what is said tends to be true and literal. If Francesca had heeded the words spoken in her first nightmare, she would have saved herself months of grief. But then again, as we know from experience, love is blind—and a journey, rather than a destination.

NIGHTMARE

Non-Literal Warning, Example #3:
An Overpowering Invasion

Warnings often happen as a series of dreams, as it did for Candace. Nightmares about her new boyfriend inspired Candace to make a critical decision.

A Break-In

Candace had a nightmare about a thug in a black leather jacket who comes onto her property and parks several strange cars in her driveway; the gangster leaves before she can tell him to get out. But a while later, he returns with his gang and ignores her requests to leave. Candace woke up disturbed and frightened: it was a story about intimidation and being invaded.

Analysis: Candace had a new boyfriend and had been having second thoughts about their relationship. He was a bit of a bully and she didn't like his overbearing manner. Sometimes he rudely ordered her around, and, to keep the peace, Candace complied. Her nightmare warned: "He's taking over; protect yourself."

On the Brink of a Huge Eruption

In a second nightmare, Candace is cleaning a room and sees a large spider on a wall, its sac swollen and about to burst. Candace is terrified of spiders and knows from the swollen sac that it is about to spawn many more scary creatures and create a horrible mess. She resolves to kill the spider. As Candace moves forward, a second one appears and as she moves forward, they both vanish. Candace cannot get rid of the spiders.

Analysis: The nightmare was a story about something scary that was about to escalate. Her new boyfriend was prone to temper tantrums, and Candace recognized the second nightmare as a warning. After her boyfriend had an angry outburst, he would apologize and shrug off his fiery behavior, expecting Candace to accept his bad behavior. Candace was getting tired of his see-saw behavior, at times of boyish charm and at times, a bad temper. Thanks to these warnings, Candace left and felt an immediate sense of relief. Remembering the sac of unborn spiders, Candace knew she had sidestepped a batch of unending horrors.

NIGHTMARE

Non-Literal Warning, Example #4:
A Spiritual Warning

The Dreamer: Nia was a twenty-three-year-old who took her spiritual life seriously. One morning she woke up, extremely distressed by a nightmare.

Nia had dreamed that a former college classmate, who is one of the most loving people she knows, is giving her feedback about herself. The male friend tells Nia she has changed, and not for the better, and that parts of her personality are now unpleasant, that she is no longer likeable. Though the friend speaks in a kind manner rather than an accusation, his words cut deep. Nia gulped; she knows it is true.

Analysis: A recent relationship breakup left her emotionally scarred, and instead of moving on, Nia became cynical. She pushed others away and no longer had anything good to say about anyone or anything. As a spiritual warning, the nightmare said "Hey, that's not you."

To her credit, Nia recognized the truth. Reclaiming a natural optimism, Nia let the past go and moved on to better prospects.

NIGHTMARES

Non-Literal Warning, Example #5:
The Computer Hack

The Dreamer: Like most millennials, twenty-four-year-old Benjamin was never far from electronic devices—and as every nerd knows, getting hacked is your worst nightmare. A series of nightmares mirrored Ben's three-month battle with cyber-attackers.

Compromised Boundaries

In the first nightmare, Ben sees a man on his back porch, peering into his window. His backyard has become a neighborhood sidewalk with lots of people walking by. Ben is taken aback. There should be no one on his back porch, so he tells the man at his window to go away. The stranger is defiant and confident; he smiles, somehow knowing that Ben cannot make him go away. A second man and a boy join the stranger at Ben's window. Ben shouts, telling them to go away, but they could care less. As the stranger smirks, the boy tries to get into the house by pushing through the back door. Ben pulls the boy's ears, shoves him away, and locks the door. Ben is relieved, but his relief is short-lived. The intruders have not gotten in, but they are still there, so he does not feel safe.

Analysis: Ben wakes up in terror, wondering if the dream is a warning that thieves will try to break into his house. The story is about trespassing and an attempted break-in, so Ben's thought was not that far off. However, Ben had missed an important cue: the people walking past his house on a bustling sidewalk were a tipoff—a metaphor that captured what the nightmare was about. The Internet is often called "an information highway"; although Ben didn't connect the dots till later, the nightmare was a warning about hackers who were getting too close for comfort.

Thieves Scale the Bedroom Walls

In a second nightmare, Ben watches four thugs scale the walls of his house and then break through the glass sliding doors of his bedroom to get in. He tries to fight them off, but they are too powerful. The thieves advance in serious attack mode, more resolved than ever to steal all they can. Ben is horrified; their faces are mean and evil. Ben calls the police; they cannot help. The only way to get rid of the thieves is to make a deal, so Ben makes the deal. But as an act of revenge and terror, the thugs kill someone anyway. Ben woke up in a cold sweat; the vicious attack left him puzzled.

Analysis: Though Ben was somewhat tech-savvy, a few weeks later he accidentally clicked on a malware link and his computer instantly froze as a "You Are

Hacked" message popped up on his screen. Oops. In a flash, Ben understood his nightmares. As happens to many, the hackers had demanded a ransom, posting instructions for payment and an untraceable phone number. Ben knew better than to pay the hackers, who generally take the money and run without restoring files. Ben asked local techs to clean his hard drive; for a fee, they reloaded the files. Paying the techs was the symbolic equivalent of making a deal, the killing in the dream paralleled the death of his hard drive—although thankfully his files survived. Relieved, Ben backed up files in several places and got on with his life. Until. . . . Several weeks later, Ben was unnerved by yet another nightmare.

A Major Tooth Cracks

In a third nightmare, as Ben is eating, a major tooth cracks. He says "Oh, no, that can't be," but knows the tooth is lost. In real life, Ben had recently lost a tooth and replaced it at great expense. In the nightmare, the cracked tooth falls and lands in a crevice beside the previous tooth that he had actually lost. In the dream, Ben wonders if he can just push the tooth back into place, but it's too late. He needs a new tooth.

Analysis: The nightmare was a story about an accident that reoccurs. Ben wanted to believe that the nightmare was just telling him that he needed another dental checkup, but this time he knew better. The recent computer mishap crossed his mind. Could the hackers have left an electronic trace that could re-freeze his computer? The techs who had fixed Ben's hard drive said yes, that was possible; in today's cyber world, techs could guarantee nothing. Ben took a breath. His computer was okay, for the moment, and he wanted to believe it would stay that way. Yet his gut kept whispering "Oh, no." All Ben could do was wait for the other shoe to drop—if it was going to.

It did. A few weeks later, a new message from the hackers appeared on his screen, complete with skull and crossbones, announcing that the software "key" that ran his computer was about to expire and his computer would freeze. All would be lost unless . . . blah, blah, blah. The hackers had messed with the code that ran the computer; and local techs did not know how to find or fix the problem.

Oi vey. Ben was out of options, but he was a fighter. Ben was also a believer in prayer, so he prayed, saying "God, if there is a solution, lead me to it." Then, keeping the faith, Ben let go of the struggle. Hours later, as he was working on something else, an idea crossed his mind. On a whim, Ben looked up support numbers of Microsoft techs: one number listed an immediate callback from an advanced technician, for emergency situations. Ben dialed the number and held his breath. Who was he to ask a stranger for help? Receiving the promised callback minutes later, Ben explained the key code problem and hackers' warning that his hard drive would crash in a matter of hours. Ben lucked out. Using remote support, the good-hearted superstar technician replaced the damaged code, examined the structures that ran the computer, and assured Ben that the problem was resolved. Ben gratefully thanked the tech support angel . . . and the Almighty.

Except . . . Ben had seen how vicious and persistent hackers can be, and anyone who has been hacked knows how vulnerable you feel afterward; he wondered whether there would be another dream. There was. However, this one made Ben chuckle in delight.

The Tables Are Turned

In a final nightmare, Ben looks out his back window and sees dark shadows moving in his backyard. As he looked closer, he sees a scruffy workman poking through the shrubs as if looking for something. Another man appears and does the same. Ben realizes they are intruders, so he picks up the phone and calls the police. The first intruder notices Ben, and they lock gazes. The intruder instantly knows that the jig is up and police are about to get him. Paralyzed with fear, the intruders run away as fast as they can, trying to get away.

Waking up, Ben chuckled. Along with a new key code, the Microsoft tech had left an electronic signal that turned the tables on the hackers, traced them, and deflated their dark intentions. This time, the intruders were terrified, not Ben! Having experienced the value of dream warnings, Ben knew his computer was safe at last.

IS THE NIGHTMARE LITERAL OR SYMBOLIC?

A nightmare can have all the features of a literal and true warning, yet point to an issue that simply *feels* bad. A car accident can be a true warning in a dream, or a metaphor about a negative or painful emotional impact. One mother dreamed her teenager was in a deadly car crash and had several recurring nightmares about such a crash; sadly, it did happen. Another mother saw her only child in a car crash, then rushed to the hospital; her child was okay. That mother's nightmare was a metaphor about news that her child was moving a thousand miles away because of a job offer. At a guess, less than one percent of dreams may be literal predictions; most are metaphors about your life.

No matter how scary a nightmare is, start with a story line, examine the metaphors, and see how the story may relate to your life. Take the time to figure it out. Even if it is not a literal warning, the message can be important.

Hint #1: Some Dream Types Tend to Be More Literal

The author's first book, *The Bedside Guide to Dreams*, describes twenty-seven dream types; all twenty-seven types are listed at Interpretadream.com. Of the twenty-seven, a handful tend to have a more literal thrust in message content. Let's take a few examples. ESP dreams are often literal, but dreams about winning the lottery do not tend to be literal; lottery dreams tend to be a metaphor about an accomplishment or opportunity like a promotion, finding true love, or mastering a challenge. Dreams about your health are often quite literal; they can be as clear as a doctor showing you an accurate X-ray of a physical condition or explaining the medical issue. Dreams of artists are often literal, like a musician who hears the melody of a new song, an artist who sees the colors and shapes of a new canvas, or a writer who dreams about the plot for a new book. A practice dream can advance or unfold an actual talent the dreamer has, and practice dreams are often literal. And dreams related to problem-solving often demonstrate, or hint at, an actual solution to the problem.

In a broad sense, whenever you are in the throes of an urgent situation, a dream often provides a literal glimpse into a solution or how things will turn out . . . *if* you proceed as planned. If you are about to buy a home and dream of a house with a cracked foundation, do not sign on the dotted line without a full home inspection. If you interview for a job and have a nightmare about a former, nasty boss . . . run. A still, quiet, voice—the voice of your own wiser self—often whispers actual truths, in dreams.

Hint #2: Ponder Why You Had the Dream

Another way to sift an ambiguous dream is to consider the dream's purpose. Dreams answer the secret questions and feelings that are on your mind. Examine what is on your mind. Dreams comment on hidden fears, hopes, and wishes, and give feedback on problems and emotional knots. Review what is going on in your life; review your feelings. What needs an answer or an insight? Tracing the dream backwards, to thoughts and feelings, can connect you to a story line and help you determine whether the dream message is literal or symbolic.

Hint # 3: Practice Makes Perfect

It is easier to decipher dream warnings if you analyze dreams regularly. Even if you are making a one-time attempt, when a nightmare shakes you up, try the Five-Step Method to decipher what the nightmare means.

Bonus Hint: Mystics say that you pre-dream everything *important* that eventually happens to you; that claim is particularly relevant for warning dreams.

AMBIGUOUS WARNINGS IN NIGHTMARES

NIGHTMARE

Ambiguous Warning, Example #1:
A Police Officer Dreams of Death by Gunfire

The Dreamer: Nina began training at the police academy at age twenty-one, and by twenty-three she was patrolling the streets. From the time she joined the police force, several times a year she had a recurring nightmare about patrolling a familiar street where she once had lived. Nina also felt stressed and had trouble sleeping. She wondered if she had made the right career choice.

> In a recurring nightmare, Nina sees herself on duty, patrolling Main Street on a late summer evening. She is near a Winn-Dixie grocery store and stops two white men who are driving a car with the brake lights out. She gets out of the patrol car and walks to the driver's door. As Nina approaches, the driver jumps out and shoots her twice, once in the chest, the other in the stomach. Though bleeding and

injured, Officer Nina feels no pain; she punches the driver in the face and handcuffs him. The other man tries to run away on foot. As Nina chases him, he fires two shots: one hits her in the stomach. Nina drives herself to the hospital and receives emergency surgery, but dies a week later from complications. In the dream, Nina knows she is in her mid-twenties when she dies. During the dream, Nina feels at peace; she has done the world a favor by apprehending the criminals. However, she wakes up feeling terrified, her heart racing.

Story Line: Someone who faces a great challenge comes close to destruction, rallies, but in the end is overcome.

Key Symbols:

ON DUTY, ON PATROL: Doing one's duty, fulfilling one's role.

BROKEN BRAKE LIGHT: What needs repair; a signal that something needs to be fixed.

GETTING SHOT: Can be an actual warning, or a metaphor about stress that leads to change.

A VALIANT FIGHT: Dreamer's true intentions; how she sees role, her profession.

IN PURSUIT, ALTHOUGH SHOT: Overcoming the odds, doing what one must, no matter what.

DEATH DUE TO COMPLICATIONS: Death is a symbol of change; death due to complications hints at a change that happens for related reasons, like a side effect.

Major Life Issues, in Dreamer's Own Words: "Not sure about my career choice. I wonder if the pressure and negative parts of the job are more than I can handle. Do these dreams predict I will get shot and die?"

Analysis, Addressed to the Dreamer: The dream suggests that on the job, you rise to the occasion and do well. The end of a dream often points to the answer. In this ending, you die; death often relates to a major change. Since you are in your mid-twenties when you die, the ending implies you will stay at the police force at least until your mid-twenties. After that, whether by choice or due to injury or another reason, the dream hints that you may change careers.

The nightmare has elements of a true warning: it repeats, there are intense emotions, true-to-life details, and appropriate actions and reactions by characters. So there is a possibility that the dream predicts you may encounter a confrontation of that nature, a traffic stop or a service call that first appears routine, yet unfolds into something serious that leads to injuries. With this recurring dream, it may be wise to at least consider another profession by age twenty-five.

Some may suggest it could be your fate to die young, as a true warning. However, having a warning dream does not mean the depicted fate is set in stone. Warning dreams show what can happen—if . . . *and only if*—you continue on your present path. If you are vigilant on the job or take a desk job, or change careers, the outcome can change.

As an extra consideration, here is a pop psychology thought. If you have to ask whether police work is right for you, you may have answered your own question. When something feels right, there is no need to ask. On the other hand, sometimes you grow into a challenging life path over time, so you are the only one who can answer that question. Sometimes only you, the dreamer, can fathom the truth—whether the message is a whisper about an actual date with danger, or mirrors an emotional tug-of-war about being a good police officer in a world that does not always appreciate your efforts.

Ambiguous Warning, Example #2:
My House Is On Fire

The Dreamer: At age forty-three, Dana's life and career was in good shape, and since all was on track, she was puzzled by a recurring nightmare.

The Nightmare Told in the Dreamer's Own Words:

"The past few nights, I keep dreaming that my house is on fire. I wake up very frightened."

Story Line: Someone is confronted by destruction that can quickly overwhelm.

Key Symbols:

HOUSE: As metaphor, a house has many possibilities. It can represent your body as a structure that holds you together. Or a house can be a metaphor about feeling safe, either in general or related to a specific issue.

FIRE: In this dream, what can get out of control and cause destruction.

REPEATEDLY SEEING A HOUSE ON FIRE: A strong warning that something needs attention, whether now or in the near future.

Analysis: The nightmare tells a story about something that can get out of control very quickly, destroying everything it touches. It opens up questions about what is urgent in your life and what could potentially get out of control and be destructive. Though you are the only one who can decide, here are a few possibilities, in theory, of issues that can match the story.

* *Health:* Health concerns can veer out of control and cause damage. If you or anyone around you is complaining about health symptoms, it can be a good idea to check them out.

* *Work and Career:* A house can represent security, which can reference financial or career concerns. Are there signals at work, like the company doing poorly, which could lead to layoffs or closing down? Nightmares can signal job losses or changes that affect your security.

* *Relationship Issues:* Security can also relate to personal relationships. Look for signs that a family member may be off track, like acting distant, working late, being away a lot, or a child's failing grades. Is a child or teenager being traumatized by a bully, or be taking part in secret activities like taking drugs or alcohol that could bring serious trouble?

* *Bottom Line:* Only you can determine what may need serious attention in your life, now or later. A warning nightmare often arrives in time to help. Look for signs of what may need your help and take action, as you can.

Bonus Hint—Time Frames of Warning Dreams: Some warning dreams are about the present, and some are about what is looming on the horizon. When a story line does not seem to apply to you or to a situation or person around you, consider the possibility that it cites what is on the horizon. Keep an eye out for future situations that mimic the story.

Ambiguous Warning, Example #3:
A Cheating Husband

The Dreamer: Forty-year-old Tess loved being a high school teacher. All seemed well, except for a recurring nightmare about her husband that left her feeling insecure.

The Nightmare Told in the Dreamer's Own Words:

> "I have a recurring nightmare that my husband has a relationship with another woman. I wake up feeling devastated."

Story Line: Someone sees another not living up to their commitment.

Key Symbols:

HUSBAND: Can be the actual husband. Or in a woman's dream, a male figure can be a symbol of her own strength.

ANOTHER WOMAN: Can reference an actual person or stranger, or symbolize the dreamer.

FEELING DEVASTATED: A warning; a reaction that invites the dreamer to investigate what would make her feel that way as it relates to someone around her, or her own actions or state of mind.

Analysis: The scene is simple and straightforward, yet the message can be difficult to pinpoint. Let's scan the possibilities.

* *What Is On Someone's Mind.* Though most dreams are symbolic, nightmares can be a true warning about what is going on, or what someone may be considering.

* *Issues About Strength.* A male in a woman's dream, such as a husband, can represent your strengths, as the ability to take the initiative or to assert yourself. If that were the case, the story might flag a betrayal to yourself in some way, like a bad habit that weakens you. Or it can highlight issues of unused strength or initiative, becoming passive, as an abdication of your potentials. Is there something you want to do, now or in your past, such as being a school counselor or principal, that you may have pushed away? If so, the dream could invite you to reconsider such goals.

* *Feelings to Confront.* You mention feeling insecure as a life issue. If insecurity is a long-time issue, the nightmare can be an invitation to deal with those feelings. Like a doctor trying to lance a wound, the psyche can at times trigger an insecurity in a dream, so that you can name it and deal with it.

Bottom Line: Recurring nightmares are a knock on the door about something important that needs attention. Husbands can stray. You can stray from hopes, goals, and standards. Dreams are about you; as you evaluate options with honesty, you can discover what is true.

CHAPTER SIX

Recurring Nightmares

A recurring nightmare is an urgent message that knocks at your awareness until the message gets through. Deep down you know when intense pain is poking at you, pain that you'd rather ignore. Pushing pain away is a coping mechanism we all understand, but it does not resolve the issue. Once you take the bull by the horns and confront what hurts, hiding behind a recurring nightmare, you can lance a wound which, left untreated, may slowly poison feelings and personality. A woman who was raped as a child cannot fully love as an adult until she acknowledges the pain and lets it heal. A man who was abandoned by his father as a teenager must deal with feelings of rejection before he can feel whole. Viewed that way, a recurring nightmare can be a gift that transforms.

AN EXCLAMATION POINT

A recurring nightmare is the equivalent of an exclamation point; it is a scream that shouts: *Pay attention! You have to deal with this!* When an urgent message does not get through, scenes become more extreme. The guns get bigger, the explosions get louder, and more people die—until the intensity becomes unbearable. Extreme gets your attention.

COPING AND REPRESSION

In psychology, a coping mechanism refers to the mental and emotional tools you use to deal with pain and challenge. When you put pain or challenge on hold, the pushing-away is called a defense or a coping mechanism. People have different ways to cope. Two people lose a beloved spouse. A man who lost his wife may never speak about her; he keeps all of his pain inside. A woman who lost her husband may talk nonstop about her departed loved one. They have opposite ways of dealing with the loss, yet both are coping mechanisms.

A period of silence can bring healing; pushing pain away builds a wall that keeps feelings at bay. However, some people get too good at repressing their pain and end up inhibiting all their feelings, not just the painful ones. You can shove feelings so far back that they never heal—and, like a festering wound, the pain comes back to haunt you. Years later, a song, a movie, or something someone says re-opens the wound, and in a flash, all hell breaks loose: they have an emotional breakdown. It happens. A recurring nightmare shouts "Deal with the pain before it sneaks up on you and explodes."

HINTS ABOUT RECURRING NIGHTMARES

Though it may seem obvious, key features about recurring nightmares may surprise you.

* *The Same Story:* Recurring nightmares can be an exact repetition every time, of the same story. Or the story line can be similar but show up with different symbols and metaphors.

* *A Jolt:* A recurring nightmare can pack an emotional punch that shocks you into paying attention.

* *A Link to an Experience:* A recurring nightmare often links back to a traumatic experience or a dramatic episode, which felt overwhelming at the time.

* *Explore the Timing:* Nightmares often begin soon after a trauma; try to determine when the nightmares began. Traumatic memories can remain dormant for months or years as a form of repression; nightmares about the issue can begin later, triggered by an incident that reminds the dreamer of the original experience. Explore what the triggering event reminds you of; it may point you to the source of the pain.

* *Embrace Transformation:* If you find the message behind a recurring nightmare and find ways to heal the original painful event, emotional blocks begin to release. If the painful event was recent, healing can be quick. When recurring nightmares relate to a trauma from years ago, the pain can take time to heal.

VARIETIES OF RECURRING NIGHTMARES

As covered in the previous chapter, repeating nightmares can be a warning. This chapter examines a recurring nightmare as a statement about pain as relates to a specific experience. The painful event may go back a long time like a childhood trauma, or relate to a recent experience like a rape, loss due to a flood or hurricane, or any experience that feels life-shattering.

The recurring nightmares of teenagers deserve a separate glance, and there are examples in this chapter. Due to their age, most teenagers lack experience and have fewer coping skills, which make teens more vulnerable to emotional distress. As a result, when life serves up pain, it can feel overwhelming, making teenagers more prone to nightmares.

The following descriptions do not cover all possibilities, yet can be a useful compass to understand a wide range of recurring nightmares.

RECURRING NIGHTMARES THAT ORIGINATE IN A DISTANT, PAST, EXPERIENCE

A common source of recurring nightmares is a difficult past experience, even one the dreamer may have forgotten.

NIGHTMARE

Recurring Nightmare from Distant Past, Example #1:
Good Intentions Gone Bad

The Dreamer: Repression—pushing pain away—is a short-term coping solution. If not dealt with, pain can fester and an emotional wall can smother all feelings. That is what happened to twenty-four-year-old Tyler, a young man who felt like a robot, going through the motions as he went through each day.

Tyler had a frequent, recurring nightmare about a kind, elderly man, who walks him safely to his car. But as soon as Tyler gets to his car, a vicious clown attacks. Fearing for his life, Tyler escapes the clown's attacks, yet wakes up terrified.

Analysis: The nightmares suggested that Tyler had two emotional tracks inside of him. Inside Tyler was a secure emotional part where life felt safe, as seen in the old man. Tyler also had a vulnerable, terrified emotional streak, seen in the attacking clown, who was probably a link to a past trauma. The nightmares were a wake-up call about something that still terrified Tyler. By taking the time to seek help to understand his nightmares, Tyler won life's lottery: he found a dream analyst who was also a therapist and helped him heal a deep wound.

NIGHTMARE

Recurring Nightmare from Distant Past, Example #2:
An Intruder Kills My Mom

The Dreamer: At age thirty, Rebecca examined a recurring nightmare that she had been having from the ages of seven to sixteen. Though the nightmares had stopped, she needed to know what they meant.

In the nightmare, Rebecca is in her room and hears an intruder. She goes to her mother's room, screams and yells, trying to warn her mother about the intruder. But her mother never hears her young daughter, so the intruder rushes in and kills her mother. Rebecca reaches for a gun to kill the intruder but the gun does not work. She runs to the neighbors; the intruder follows and kills the neighbors. Rebecca runs to the next house. The same thing happens over and over again until she wakes up, feeling petrified and helpless.

Analysis: Rebecca had a mother who, by nature, was not warm or close. Every day, as a child, her mother's coldness made Rebecca feel terrified and abandoned, emotions the nightmare replayed. Trying to save her mother paralleled Rebecca's daily childish attempt to win her mother's love and affection. Rebecca could never succeed.

At age sixteen, Rebecca's recurring nightmares stopped. That was when she found her feet and carved out an independent path. Young ones cannot understand the mental or emotional turmoil that a parent may experience, such as abuse, mental illness, or alcohol or drug use—situations that make parents shut down and become distant. All a child knows is that the adult is not there for them. Angels—heavenly ones or people in the community—sometimes help young ones like Rebecca to uncover their own strength. Rebecca was emotionally rescued by a neighbor's warm smile and an occasional after-school visit with the neighbor that featured milk, cookies, and a caring ear. Take note: a small kindness can save a child's life.

NIGHTMARE

Recurring Nightmare from Distant Past, Example #3:
A Plane Crash Kills My Family

Here is a detailed example of a recurring nightmare that began in childhood:

The Dreamer: Marsha was a fifty-five-year-old whose mother had died two years earlier; in personality, Marsha was normally serious and dutiful. As she inched into her senior years, she wanted to discover the lighthearted, joyful energy of childhood; as one part of her journey of self-exploration, Marsha started monitoring her dreams. However, instead of encountering happy dreams of childhood scenes, Marsha had a series of startling, recurring nightmares.

The Recurring Nightmare, Told in the Dreamer's Own Words:

"We were on a plane taking off. The plane had two levels. My daughter and I were on the top level, the rest of my large family and my dead mother were on the bottom level. A few minutes after takeoff, the plane decelerates, tilts toward the ground, and begins to drop. My daughter and I look out the window, watching in dread, as the wing hits the ground and the plane explodes. I grab my daughter and hold her close to me, to protect her. I cannot open the emergency exit. I become frantic. I do not see the rest of my family, but my daughter and I are okay! It feels so real!!!!! I feel a giant sadness come over me and wake up feeling lost. I want to cry."

Story Line: Someone experiences disaster with loved ones; some survive, but most do not.

Key Symbols:

AIRPLANE WITH TWO LEVELS: Levels of the mind that the dreamer is exploring, as what is conscious and what is unconscious, the real and the unknown.

HIT THE GROUND AND EXPLODE: A sudden turn for the worse, an unexpected disaster.

DEATH OF FAMILY: Great loss and pain that cannot be changed or prevented.

SURVIVING A PLANE CRASH: Metaphor for transformation and survival.

DAUGHTER: An image of the dreamer's younger self, the part she is trying to reconnect to.

PROTECTING HER DAUGHTER: How dreamer survived and protected herself in her youth.

Analysis—Said Directly to the Dreamer: "The fact that you are trying to reconnect with your inner child hints that you had a difficult childhood. The metaphor of a family that dies in a crash suggests a childhood that lacked the innocence, ease, and joy associated with growing up in a normal, loving family. In your mature years you are trying to regain a lost childhood. As you reach back into your old memories, you reconnect to the pain and trauma of your youth. The sudden crash and multiple deaths suggest a history of violent family patterns and disturbances, physical or emotional, during childhood. The dream about flying, as a metaphor of rising above something, hints that as a child, you desperately wanted to escape the situation. But all you could do was learn how to protect yourself, and you did. You survived, but the emotional scars remain. At some level you grew up feeling like an orphan; you felt as if you had lost your family and your childhood. And in a sense, you did.

"In the recurring nightmares, you re-live your loss and sadness, yet you also reconnect to your childhood self. Your daughter is the younger you—the inner child that you now want to cherish. As you reach out to your daughter to love and protect her, you re-bond with the traumatized inner child of your youth. You reach out to the girl you once were, seeking a light-hearted self, but she is still full of pain. Before you can experience the childlike joy of which you were deprived, you must first heal the scars of a childhood that was a harrowing ordeal."

Marsha's Response: "You described my childhood. I see the dreams more clearly now. Thank you. Those nightmares have been haunting me for a very long time."

RECURRING NIGHTMARES LINKED TO A RECENT EVENT

A current event can trigger recurring nightmares. Nightmares can begin when an incident ends, or can pop up while the event is still happening. Once a nightmare shows up, the sooner the dreamer gets the message, the easier it can be to prevent an emotional knot.

Recurring Nightmare from a Recent Event, Example #1:
Gang-Raped and Stabbed

The Dreamer: Not yet married, twenty-four-year-old Tiana became a nervous wreck when her boyfriend began to hang out with gang members who were involved with drugs and violence. The gang members often spent time at their home.

> For weeks Tiana had a nightmare in which she sees her boyfriend get violently beaten up, then her boyfriend is forced to watch as she is gang-raped and beaten. Each nightmare ends the same way: Tiana and her boyfriend are violently stabbed, and Tiana wakes up screaming.

Analysis: The severe nightmares mirrored Tiana's fears that things could end badly. The gang members terrified Tiana, with good reason; their illegal activities could get everyone in trouble, including Tiana, just by being associated with them. Duh. Could the nightmare be any clearer? The recurring dream addressed Tiana's legitimate fears and screamed "Girl, get out of there!"

Recurring Nightmare from a Recent Event, Example #2:
Stalked By My Abusive Ex

The Dreamer: Eva was a beautiful twenty-five-year-old. During college, she had a four-year relationship with a man whose smooth charm alternated with angry episodes of physical and emotional abuse. Eva finally had the strength to walk away but was left with terrifying nightmares.

The Recurring Nightmare, Told in the Dreamer's Own Words:

"It has been two years since we broke up, but every night I still have nightmares about my abusive ex. In every nightmare he is stalking me. Everywhere I turn, he is there, forcing himself back into my life and hurting my newborn son to the point of almost killing my son, out of hate. I try to run and get away, but each time, I fail. All of a sudden I see myself back in college where I met him. Dread overtakes me, I feel like a useless failure. I relive every a part of the four-year relationship, every sad, hurtful, and painful moment. I wake up terrified, feeling pain and sorrow. I hate myself and cry."

Story Lines: Someone is constantly confronted by what overwhelms them. Someone relives their past.

Key Symbols:

ABUSIVE EX: The actual person; a symbol of traumatic memories that plague the dreamer.

STALKING: Something unwanted that keeps holding on.

NEWBORN SON: Symbol of new strength and life the dreamer began by ending the relationship.

BACK IN COLLEGE: Scene of a past emotional place.

DREAD, FEELING LIKE A FAILURE: Pinpoints the emotional scars left by the trauma.

Analysis, Said Directly to the Dreamer: "The recurring nightmares mirror the deep, unhealed, emotional leftovers from your experience with an abusive ex. You wake up hating yourself as if it were your fault, even though you were a victim: you did not bring this on yourself; abuse is never warranted. One function of dreaming is to act like a digestion system. As you relive those feelings in the nightmares, at some level you can slowly digest the fear, dread, and helplessness that you once experienced. As you digest those feelings, these scenes should become less scary and less frequent.

"However, your nightmares have not become less scary or frequent; instead, you relive the exact same episodes, over and over again. That says the scars run too deep; they cannot heal on their own. It took strength to end the relationship; you should be proud of yourself for walking away. Nevertheless, the ongoing, severe nightmares and your feelings of guilt and shame suggest that a therapist is a good idea. You were the victim, not the guilty party; you do not need to carry the pain. Enlist the help of a caring professional and free yourself."

RECURRING NIGHTMARES ABOUT A SPECIFIC CHALLENGE

Challenges like divorce, failure, losing a job, or fears about retirement, which feel like hitting a brick wall, can trigger nightmares.

NIGHTMARE

Recurring Nightmare Related to a Specific Challenge, Example #1:
The Scary Stranger

As a small-town girl, Bonnie kept dreaming that she was in a big city, living in a new apartment. A stranger keeps knocking on her door, and although she never sees who it is, the knocks terrify her. In real life, Bonnie was about to relocate to a new city and was excited about the change, so the nightmares did not make sense.

Analysis: However, even a positive change like a relocation and promotion can harbor hidden fears. Bonnie's nightmares said "You are excited; but you are also anxious about taking on more responsibility and making new friends." The scary stranger in Bonnie's nightmare was a metaphor of what she feared, as fears parked at her doorstep. As a coping mechanism, sometimes you screen out the bad stuff and focus only on the good, but hidden anxiety bounces back and shows up in a nightmare. By accepting unclaimed fear alongside the excitement, Bonnie zoomed forward into a smooth transition.

NIGHTMARE

Recurring Nightmare Related to a Specific Challenge, Example #2:
Who Stole My Car?

The Dreamer: At age fifty-nine, the company Jackson worked for downsized; he lost his job and had serious trepidation about his approaching retirement. Jackson feared that at his age, employers would pay less and prefer younger blood. Fear brings on nightmares.

> Every night, Jackson began to dream that he has lost or misplaced his car; stranded, he would wake up feeling desperate and terrified.

Analysis: The recurring nightmare mirrored real fears; yet by naming those fears, David kept his feelings under control. Dream messages do not always resolve an issue. Sometimes, like a safety valve, they help you channel and digest distress.

NIGHTMARE

Recurring Nightmare Related to a Specific Challenge, Example #3:
Drowning in a Sinking Ship

The Dreamer: By age forty-four, David had established an excellent career and home life. Nevertheless, he began to feel that something was missing, but he could not name what that was. David ignored his emotional impasse and soldiered on. However, he could not ignore the recurring nightmare that popped up.

A Recurring Nightmare, Told in the Dreamer's Own Words:

> "I am walking on a beach with a friend, talking and laughing. On the boardwalk, we see diving boards that reach into the ocean; hundreds of people line up and dive into the water. My friend follows them and dives in, so I feel compelled to do the same. No one has trouble breathing underwater. I catch up to my friend, and we swim for a long time in the same direction. We see a large cruise ship at the bottom of the ocean and everyone swims toward it. My friend and others swim

through an opening. I hurry to catch up; but when I get there, a door shuts and stops me from following; apparently, I am supposed to find my own door to swim through. I find another opening and go through it. There is a glass tunnel inside the cruise ship, and I see the others through the glass walls. I wave and make as much noise as I can, but they do not notice me. Seconds later, a door closes behind me; I am now stuck in the glass tube. I watch as others on the other side of the glass slide out of their tube and go wherever it leads. But my tunnel leads nowhere and a glass pane blocks my exit. Suddenly the water in my tunnel begins to drain. I am in an aquatic coffin, and I can no longer breathe. Everyone else swims to a safe place on the ship but I am left there to drown. I wake up, terrified, gasping for air."

Story Line: Even though someone does exactly what others do, instead of achieving the same goals, they reach a dead end.

Key Symbols:

SHIP: The ship of life, the journey of life.

SWIMMING AND FOLLOWING OTHERS: Going with the flow, behaving as others expect.

TRAPPED: Immobile, reaching a dead end.

SUFFOCATING: No longer getting what you need to survive.

Analysis: "The story suggests you did everything right in life, and did everything that was expected of you. Nevertheless, you feel stifled and are not achieving the happiness or goals you once expected. Death is often a metaphor for change. The image of suffocating says that the time has arrived when you must choose a new direction, or wither away. The end of a story often contains a hint of what to do. The ending says:

instead of following others, redefine what is meaningful to you; create a new inner compass based on what is real for you. Dreams often exaggerate to make a point. The recurring nightmare says: You have reached a dead end—change paths."

David said: "That actually makes sense. Thank you."

TEENAGERS' RECURRING NIGHTMARES ARE UNIQUE

What a teenager feels and experiences can get confusing and scary, which can bring on more nightmares than loved ones realize. Teens are unique. Here are a few observations based on dreams that teens emailed the author at Interpretadream. com, as hints that concerned parents, teachers, and adults can check out.

1. *The Physical Landscape.* Hormonal changes in teenagers precipitate intense feelings, so teenage nightmares can be intense with extreme story lines.

2. *Coping Skills.* Teens have little or no life experience, so any challenge can feel scary. Whether the issue is large, such as a teen's sexual orientation, or small, like not getting the attention of a cute boy or a pretty girl—an issue can feel overwhelming. When you pair the need to handle what is new with few coping skills, any obstacle can make a teenager feel as if their whole world is falling apart, whether for a few minutes, or forever.

3. *Sensitive and Caring Is Good.* Like adults, teens vary in personality. Add a thin or thick layer of sensitivity to the mix, and a teenager's threshold for pain can be quite low. A school test or someone's harsh words can launch bad dreams, while serious challenges like bullying

or an abusive parent can create blood-curdling, repetitive nightmares.

4. *Good Things Can Be Bad, Too.* Achievements also create stress; teens do not have experience handling the good stuff, either. Getting good grades or earning a trophy can create a silent pressure to live up to a standard a teen has not yet defined or owned. Anxiety can be a hidden side effect of a positive event, too, as unrecognized stress that creates a nightmare.

5. *To Do or Not to Do—A Concept Versus Its Application.* Adults at times forget that teens do not yet fully grasp how concepts like patience, thinking things through, or communicating relate to choices. Knowing the dictionary definition of the word "patience" is different from knowing how to be patient. Knowing how to drive a car is radically different from being able to ignore peer pressure and not drive under the influence. Making a good choice requires a level of understanding that is often beyond a teenager who instinctively feels no fear, and is not in touch with limits—their own, or the limits that life can impose.

6. *Learning a Value Versus Internalizing It.* Telling the truth is a value that you learn from parents and society. However, in psychology, "internalizing" a concept is the ability to apply what you know, like telling the truth or not driving drunk—when no one is looking. Teens can know a lot but do not always internalize what they know into habits or standards—at least not yet. The gap between knowing and internalizing makes it harder for a teenager to pair a choice with its consequence, which makes teens vulnerable to poor choices.

7. *Navigating a Challenging, Complex World.* Whether challenges that teens face are normal or extreme, conflict and distress can create blood-curdling nightmares. Since age fifteen, seventeen-year-old Leo had nightmares about a vicious attack. At first, the recurring dream featured a large black wolf that charged at Leo as he walked down his street. Leo always ran and either got home, or to a friend's house, before the wolf caught him. But he woke up terrified. After several years, instead of a wolf, a vicious dog charged at Leo. By age seventeen, in a final nightmare, Leo stopped running and faced his attacker. When the attacking dog reached Leo, the dog just stood there. It barked, snarled, was hostile and menacing, but the dog did not harm Leo.

Though strong in spirit, Leo had his mother's smaller build and intellectual inclinations, unlike his two brothers, who were football heroes like their dad. Leo had ambitious career goals and strove for high grades to get into college. The added stress of his dad's playful yet constant jabs about a lack of athletic ability and about being different was not helpful. Leo's nightmares hinted that he felt vulnerable, yet he always found a safe space to which he could retreat. Did the wolf attacks mirror the stress or pain Leo felt, when his father challenged who he was? That answer was—it does not matter. Nightmares highlighted Leo's fragile confidence; however, by age seventeen, Leo felt secure enough to face his fears. Facing his dream attacker showed a turning point: by standing his ground, Leo became comfortable with who he was. The final nightmare showed how Leo had taken a giant step in confidence and claimed a new maturity.

Examples of a Teenager's Recurring Nightmares:
Shootings and Killings

The Dreamer: As a loving grandmother, Annalise was concerned about the nightmares that her fifteen-year-old granddaughter Kate had experienced three nights in a row. After Kate's third nightmare, Kate called her grandmother at five o'clock in the morning, crying hysterically. Annalise said: "I don't know what is going on with my granddaughter; it scares me."

Kate had three recurring nightmares:

1. Kate's baby cousin is shot by a neighbor child. Kate is terrified.

2. Someone phones Kate's house, but when she answers, the caller is silent. Kate looks out the window and sees someone with a gun trying to kill her and her grandfather. She wakes up trying to scream.

3. In the third nightmare, Kate sees her grandmother Annalise on a murderous rampage. Her grandmother shoots a group of strangers that neither of them knows. Kate wakes up, hysterical, and calls her grandmother at five in the morning.

Story Lines: The nightmares share common themes: scary, unexplained messages; attacks and attackers; unexpected death and destruction. The phone calls tell a story about confusion and vulnerability, the attacks talk about feeling overwhelmed, and the killings speak of forced changes.

Key Symbols:

A CHILD KILLS A BABY COUSIN: Unexplained actions that hurt the young; a metaphor of the teen's confusing emotions.

SILENT PHONE CALLER: Hidden, scary intentions and motives, a metaphor of confusion and fear.

GRANDMOTHER AND GRANDFATHER: People the dreamer loves and feels loved by; metaphor for what makes the teen feel safe and secure, yet which is threatened in the dream.

GUN: Something potentially dangerous that can get out of control; mirrors teen's feelings.

SHOOTING AND GETTING SHOT: Death as change, changes in life that feel overwhelming.

DEATH: Generally a symbol of a huge change.

KILLING: Metaphor for changes imposed on another without their consent.

Expert's Analysis: As a wonderful teen with a big heart, Kate excelled in all she did. Her mom had just given birth to a second daughter. Kate deeply loved her new baby sister. As family and grandparents welcomed the new baby, everyone forgot that Kate was still a vulnerable teenager. She had intense, hidden, and likely unconscious angst about what life would mean now that she had a baby sister. Kate could not put feelings and questions into words; yet at a gut level she wondered how she would fit into the new world order that had been thrust upon her. The nightmares flagged Kate's confusion and unexpressed fears. By consulting a dream expert, Kate's grandmother helped Kate to name and resolve her unconscious fears. Once her fears were unraveled, Kate felt at peace.

Find more examples of teenage nightmares in the chapters that follow, flagged as dreams of teens.

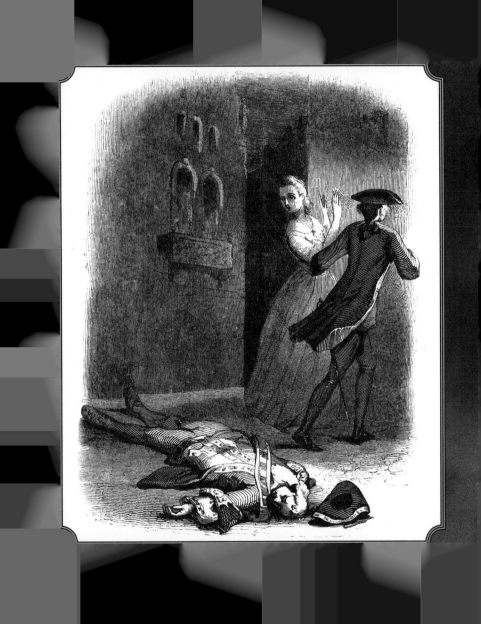

CHAPTER SEVEN

Death in Dreams

Nothing is more unnerving than a nightmare about the death of a child, a mate, or yourself. Because dreams exaggerate to get a point across, most scenes about a car accident, a plane crash, or a violent death are metaphors—though in rare cases they can be a true warning. Yet, like all dreams, even nightmares about death and dying that shake you up carry a helpful message. This chapter on death in dreams includes a discussion about what happens after death, known to some as the afterlife, the hereafter, or the sweet bye and bye.

DEATH AS A METAPHOR

Death and dying span a wide range of meanings, as in this sample list.

* *Death as Change.* Even though there are many modern accounts of near-death experiences which provide a glimpse into what happens after you die and confirm there is little to fear, many fear death as the ultimate change we will ever encounter. As a result, the most common metaphor for death is change, as a huge change related to whatever issue a dream may flag.

* *Gaming and Death.* Recent generations have grown up playing video games where killing and escaping death is an on-screen sport. Gamers may be less affected by violent clashes in nightmares; to gamers, death may be a metaphor about overcoming obstacles.

* *Strength.* If you lose your emotional strength, which can happen in the face of a huge challenge, it can feel as if you have died. Dreams of dying can mirror depleted emotional reserves.

* *Preparing for Death.* The elderly and those who are seriously ill often have dreams that prepare them for the hereafter. A deceased loved one may show up in a dream as a reassurance that they will not be alone when the time comes. In some preparation dreams, a dead loved one takes their hand and leads them away. Other images can show a person crossing a bridge, a distant place that beckons, or a door that leads into a new space.

* *Saying Goodbye.* After a loved one dies, the deceased often appears in a dream as if to say hello or goodbye. Such dreams typically happen soon after their death, but can take place even years later.

DEATH AS A HEADS-UP ABOUT
A CHALLENGE

Although dreams about death are often about change, death can at times also be a heads-up about an upcoming obstacle or challenge. A change related to the future implies that the psyche is aware of an upcoming event. Does that mean ESP in dreams is real? Maybe, but let's leave that question for another day. Instead, consider the author's theory of how decisions relate to the warnings about the future, in dreams.

Seeing the Big Picture as a Form of ESP

Suppose a decision is like a soccer ball, perched at the top of a hill, that you are ready to kick down the hill. From the top, you see stones on one side, smooth grass on the other, and a stream with rocks in the middle of the hill. When it comes to dreams, your psyche—the part of you that connects you to all that you think, feel, and do—stands at the top of the hill of your awareness. Every time you take action or ponder what you may do, the psyche sends a test ball down the hill—like a practice kick. The test ball is an educated guess about the result— namely, where the ball will land and what obstacles the ball will face before it lands. Such simulations by the psyche track the potentials and consequences of important actions, feelings, and thoughts. And once the psyche has a best-guess scenario, you receive a dream e-mail of what might happen, as a report to your waking self.

Place Your Bets

In essence, a warning dream is a message from your asleep self to your awake self, about the projected effect of an action, idea, question, or feeling. When you get a heads-up in a dream, like placing a bet, the dream message says: "If you stay on this course and bet on this pony, this is the likely result." *But* . . . if you change directions, actions, or thoughts, the results can change—and that is an important point! Like brakes on a car, in most cases a warning dream is an encouragement to evaluate your actions, decisions, thoughts, and feelings, and, if necessary, to change them. If you are curious about how a dream is born and how a dream unfolds, you can find a more detailed explanation in the author's earlier book, *A Little Bit of Dreams.*

NIGHTMARES ABOUT DEATH

This chapter explains four main tracks about nightmares that deal with death and dying, and continues with an in-depth discussion about each track, with examples.

1. *Death as Positive Change.* Death in a dream can highlight positive change.

2. *Endings or Painful Change.* Dying can be a metaphor about a painful, negative ending or change.

3. *Grief.* Many dreams about death mirror actual loss and grief.

4. *Visits by the Dead.* Dreams can show an actual visit from someone who has died.

DEATH AS A MESSAGE ABOUT POSITIVE CHANGE

Most dreams about death relate to change. To pinpoint the change, create a story line and match the story to a situation, an attitude, a goal, or a feeling. The first clue about what death means, in a dream, is your emotions.

Death as Positive Change, Example #1:
You Have Two Months to Live

The Dreamer: At fifty-eight, Tom was in good health, all was well with his family, and his career was on track.

Life felt good, so he was puzzled when he had a nightmare about an announcement that he had two months to live. As he woke up, Tom wondered if he was about to die. Tom became even more puzzled because, in the dream, the news about dying felt exciting.

Analysis: This story about dying referred to an ending, and in this case the ending made Tom feel good. As he considered dying as a metaphor about endings, Tom saw two possible changes on the horizon, both work-related. He could take a promotion that was on the table, a job that came with travel and a bump in salary. Or, he could take an early retirement package that his company was offering him and others in his age group. Because of Tom's happy feelings, the nightmare said "In two months, you will die to the life you now lead." Decide which change feels right. Who knew that a dream about dying could make you happy? Tom did.

Death as Positive Change, Example #2:
What Lies Beyond the Grave

The Dreamer: Some teenage dreams have positive messages, like this dream about a graveyard. Grace was a fifteen-year-old who balanced a hectic life as an honors student, volunteer work, and a part-time job. She had no complaints. However, as a spiritual seeker, Grace wanted to explore the deeper meaning of life.

The Dream, Told in Dreamer's Own Words:

"I was standing up in a grave. As I looked up at the clear blue sky, I could see the sides of the grave with soil piled high around the edges. It felt peaceful, like a meditation. I woke up feeling very calm. I felt uplifted for days."

Story Line: Though in a place that scares many, someone feels great peace.

Key Symbols:

GRAVE: A scary unknown; symbol of reaching out into the hereafter.

LOOKING AT SOIL ON EDGES OF GRAVE: Exploring where one is at, facing what could be fearful.

LOOK UP FROM THE GRAVE: Seeing what is beyond; looking past normal limits.

BLUE SKY: What is peaceful and relaxing; no troubles.

FELT LIKE A MEDITATION: Touching a deeper part of self, connecting to one's soul.

FEELING AT PEACE: Reaching an understanding; an experience of grace beyond understanding.

Analysis: At age fifteen, life can feel intense. Because Grace sincerely sought spiritual meaning, a dream about death offered her a glimpse into eternity. The peace that Grace experienced in a grave was a connection to death and the hereafter, a connection that let her savor the deeper spirituality she sought. Seeing beyond the grave was an invitation for Grace to own her personal spiritual journey. It could also have been a hint to meditate; many say that meditation provides a slice of peace and calm that helps meet life's challenges.

DEATH AS A PAINFUL ENDING
OR CHANGE

Most scenes about death and dying are messages about painful, unpleasant changes or endings, as in these examples.

Death as a Painful Ending or Change, Example #1:
My Boyfriend Is Dead

Though some couples commit to a relationship in their younger years, many have several dance partners before they settle down.

The Dreamer: Twenty-year-old Jayla was head over heels in love; she thought nothing of bending over backward to please her boyfriend. However, they bickered a lot.

> In her nightmare, Jayla's boyfriend walks out on her, saying "To hell with this." Jayla then sees her boyfriend lying dead outside her door; his body is ice-cold. Jayla woke up crying, feeling freaked out.

Analysis: As a dream message, her boyfriend's words said it all—he was walking away—and his sudden death screamed "This relationship is about to end." Though painful, Jayla's nightmare message was an opportunity to walk away with her self-respect intact. At age twenty, she had plenty of time to find a new partner.

Death as a Painful Ending or Change, Example #2:
A Fatal Car Crash

The Dreamer: At twenty-one, Cara was madly in love, yet she feared losing her boyfriend. In a nightmare,

> Cara dreams she is watching TV at home, alone; feeling afraid to be alone, she asks her boyfriend to come over. However, he's drunk and does not want to come over. Cara insists. On his way to Cara's house, her boyfriend's car crashes and he dies instantly. Cara woke up crying, shocked at her boyfriend's sudden death.

Analysis: As a secondary issue, the fact that Cara was afraid to be alone hinted that she had insecurity issues she needed to deal with before she could establish a comfortable relationship. However, Cara's insecurity was not the main focus of the nightmare. The dream was a story about forcing another's hand, a forcing that would bring a sudden negative result. The nightmare cautioned Cara to go slow. As a metaphor about endings, the instant death warned Cara that pushing her boyfriend could backfire and bring the relationship to an abrupt end.

Death as a Painful Ending or Change, Example #3:
Killing a Dog

The Dreamer: At age thirty-five, Jeni knew her marriage was on the brink.

> A recurring nightmare about a dog that kept trying to bite her left her terrified. In the nightmare, Jeni tries to protect herself by holding

the dog's neck at arm's length, but the dog manages to bite her, anyway. Desperate to defend herself, Jeni finally kills the dog. However, as an animal lover, she wakes up ashamed of what she has done.

Analysis: As a story, the dog attacks mirrored a marriage that was in tatters and scarred by vicious verbal attacks at Jeni by her husband, with undertones of physical threats. Killing the dog was an announcement of an ending. The nightmare told a story about someone who resorts to extreme measures to defend themselves, because moderate measures had not worked. The shame Jeni felt at killing the dog suggested that she believed marriage should last forever and felt guilty that this marriage was not working. A forever marriage is great; choosing a mate with whom that can work is a separate issue. Jeni did not want to end the marriage, yet the nightmare hinted "You cannot appease your husband's rage; leaving is the only way out."

Bonus Hint: An attack can be a metaphor about anger, a common emotion when couples fight and clash. The more violent the angry attacks in a dream, the greater the anger in a relationship. And if attack scenes include death and killing, a nightmare may flash a serious relationship warning.

NIGHTMARE

Death as a Painful Ending or Change, Example #4:
A Health Warning

The Dreamer: Louise was fifty-eight. She rarely remembered her dreams, but a nightmare about her husband's death got her full attention.

> In the dream, Louise and her husband are driving and as they turn a corner, a truck crashes into their car. Louise jumps out, horrified, watching her husband die in a pool of blood.

Analysis: The nightmare gut punch describes a sudden, unexpected, disaster. As a metaphor, a car can symbolize your body as the vehicle that carries you through life. By extension, a car crash can be a heads-up about a health concern; and because it was the husband who died, the message flagged his health, saying "If your husband does not pay attention to his health, there can be dire consequences." Can a nightmare save a life? Elbowed by the dream scare, Louise was determined to try. Louise scheduled medical visits to keep an eye on her husband's high blood pressure and cast a fresh eye toward nutritious meals to dissolve the spare tire that was building up around his waist.

DEATH AS GRIEF ABOUT ACTUAL LOSS

When a loved one dies, a dream about their death can help you process your grief. Researchers Aaron Greenberg and Milton Kramer did some research that suggested one function of dreaming is to act like a digestion system for pain and distress. Their studies with war veterans revealed how story lines in dreams parallel the events in a dreamer's life and help defuse painful emotions of those with post-traumatic stress disorder (PTSD). For some, a single dream helps them deal with grief; for others, it can take many dreams.

NIGHTMARE

Death as Grief & Loss, Example #1:
Dancing the Night Away

The Dreamer: After a three-year illness, Mazie's father passed away.

A few weeks later, thirty-two-year-old Mazie dreamed she was at a reception, dancing with her deceased dad. Their relationship had not always been positive, though in the dream she loves dancing with him. Maizie wants to tell her father that she cares, despite their differences, but the dance feels too good to stop and talk. Her dad loved to dance. In fact, the first time he felt sick was while he was dancing at a party, after which he became seriously ill.

Analysis: Sometimes words get in the way. In her dream visit, Mazie and her father dance in silence, letting their mutual love speak volumes. As they dance, the grief and guilt Mazie feels about their less-than-perfect relationship evaporates.

NIGHTMARE

Death as Grief & Loss, Example #2:
Carjacked

The Dreamer: As a thirty-five-year-old mother, Chloe was devastated when her eleven-year-old son died, unexpectedly, after a brief illness. A few weeks later, the grieving mother had a nightmare about a carjacking:

> Someone steals Chloe's car, and her children and cell phone are still inside the car. Helpless and in extreme pain, all Chloe can do in the nightmare is watch the carjacker speed away.

Analysis: The nightmare told a story about losing what is most precious, with no way to stop what was happening. The story expressed Chloe's deep emotions: her son's death felt as if she had been robbed. Like ocean waves that crash against jagged rocks, the nightmare replayed the sad song in Chloe's heart to help Chloe process an unspeakable loss one day at a time.

Death as Grief & Loss, Example #3:
A Deep Wound

The Dreamer: In her mid-forties, Sarah grieved the sudden, unexpected death of her twenty- year-old daughter.

> In a nightmare, she watches her ex-husband in bed with a strange girl, rubbing his fingers through the girl's hair. To Sarah, her ex-husband's actions with the young girl feel profane, and she confronts him. Her ex-husband points to a large, fresh wound with the staples still in the wound, on the girl's head, and explains that his pats on the girl's head are an attempt to heal the wound.

Analysis: The story describes pain in need of healing and a gentle approach that accomplishes the healing. The head can be a metaphor about attitudes. And in a woman's dream, a husband can symbolize the woman's personal strength. After losing her daughter, Sarah felt depressed, lost her will to live, and allowed dark thoughts to linger. The ex-husband was a whispered metaphor about Sarah's "ex" strength—the inner strength she had lost due to grief. The message said "To regain strength, replace the dark thoughts that have entered your feelings with gentle, positive thoughts that soothe the spirit. The husband's light pats on an injured head mirrored the slow, gentle process that Sarah needed, to digest deep wounds of loss a tiny piece at a time.

Death as Grief & Loss, Example #4:
Something Special is Gone

The Dreamer: As fifty-year-old Tobias discovered, you can grieve a loss that is not an actual death. Death can also be a symbol for other life changes you may grieve.

> Since his life was on track, Tobias was shocked by a nightmare about a small gray kitten curled up in a ball, as if asleep. Tobias looks closer and notices that the kitten is limp and lifeless, as if dead, though it is not dead. Frantic, Tobias tries to save the helpless creature but cannot save it.

Analysis: As happens to many, in real life Tobias and his siblings had noticed a decline in their father's physical and mental functioning; labels like dementia and Alzheimer's were bounced around. Tobias and his dad shared a love of carpentry; they had done many projects together. It pained Tobias to see his dad recede into shadows. The half-dead kitten mirrored the grief Tobias felt at his aging father's downward trek.

`NIGHTMARE`

Death as Grief & Loss, Example #5:
A Teen Loses Her Best Friend

The Dreamer: In real life, fourteen-year-old Eliza actually witnessed her best friend get fatally hit by a train. Eliza said: "I felt awful because I couldn't save her. No matter how hard I tried, there was nothing I could do." A month later, Eliza had the following nightmare.

> In Eliza's nightmare, a big house has a lot of doors that are shut, and behind each door is a dead person. However, in that house, the dead are alive. A middle-aged woman owns the house; if someone came in, the woman does not let them go back into the real world: they are trapped there forever. Somehow Eliza enters the house and, because

she is truly alive, the woman dislikes Eliza and follows her around. Eliza finds her best friend behind one of the doors. She talks to her friend and realizes her friend cannot leave, but Eliza can. She walks around, looking for an escape route, anyway, so that they can both leave. She smashes a basement window, but the woman who owns the house sees her. Seeing that there is no way out, the friend smiles and tells Eliza it is all right to leave her behind. Eliza refuses, but in the end she sees that she must go, even though she will leave her friend stuck in the house, dead, all by herself. Eliza leaves; but when she sees she cannot get back in, she panics. She wakes up terrified and in pain because she had to leave her friend behind.

Story Line: Though someone reconnects with a loved one and tries to keep the connection, they see that they must move on.

Key Symbols:

A BIG HOUSE WITH DEAD PEOPLE: An image of the Great Beyond.

CLOSED DOORS: The unknown, what is beyond the grave.

DEAD PERSON BEHIND EACH DOOR: Metaphor for a place where the dead reside.

TRAPPED INSIDE THE HOUSE: Coming to terms with the limitations of life and death, and what separates the dead and the living.

STARTED TO PANIC: Mirrors dreamer's grief and guilt at not being able to help her friend.

FRIEND'S WORDS "IT IS ALL RIGHT TO LEAVE": A blessing from the dead friend to the dreamer.

Analysis—As Said to Dreamer: "Whatever the circumstance of the train accident, it would be unusual if you or anyone could have saved your friend, even though you wanted to. As best friends, you think of her. In your grief, your souls connected during sleep; and even though she said it was okay to leave her, the loss feels bad. The dream tells you that your friend knows you love her, and the love and friendship you shared will always be there. Your friend accepts what happened to her and confirms it is okay for you to move on. Take time to grieve, yet know that you have your friend's blessing to move on and live a happy life."

DREAM VISITS FROM THE DEAD

Although dreaming about someone who has died is a common experience, this next thought may leave you reeling: While most dreams about death are symbolic, in the author's experience a dream about a loved one who has died often depicts an actual visit by the deceased. Accepting the possibility that a dead person can visit in a dream depends on what you believe takes place after you die. The question about what happens after we die warrants a quick peek into what is called Heaven, the Afterlife, or the Hereafter.

Near-Death Experiences (NDEs)

In past centuries, clergymen, mystics, and saints were the ones who spoke about heaven and hell—other than the occasional tongue-in-cheek references by normal folks. These days, thanks to firsthand accounts about near-death experiences by individuals who died and then came back to life, many talk about heaven and the hereafter. And because of groups like IANDS (International Association for Near Death Studies) who log and disseminate such experiences on websites, anyone can evaluate thousands of shared glimpses into the hereafter.

Such glimpses into death and dying hint that life in the Great Beyond is similar, yet different, to life as we know it here on earth. When you die, what is similar to life on earth is that you reconnect with loved ones, develop talents, take on new studies, and accept tasks and responsibilities. What is different is that you function without a body and you clearly know that love and spiritual progress is the true purpose of life, both on earth—and in the hereafter. In a personal NDE, the author experienced a city made of sparkling white light, as a place where good folks go after they die, a city that radiates a perfect love that surpasses all understanding. Some might call it heaven.

Common elements of NDEs include seeing a bright light, realms of indescribable love, glimpses of God and angels, and reconnecting with deceased loved ones. A few NDEs point to darker haunts. Those who deliberately do evil may earn a ticket to a place of suffering, at least for a while. Souls in places of suffering are rescued, if and when the soul seeks Light—the light of God's perfect love and ways.

Prayers Unite the Living and the Dead

Most religious services include prayers for the dead, which are normally recited at burials. Whether someone lived a good life or not, it is a good idea to pray for those who have passed on; the dead benefit from prayer as much as do the living. A select few who die may have a more urgent need for prayer. As depicted in movies like Ghost or haunted-house stories, on extremely rare occasions a soul can get stuck on earth; such souls desperately need prayer to release themselves into the hereafter. Though rare, it may happen often enough to have earned a place in folklore.

How does a dead soul get stuck on earth? Near-death experiences suggest that someone who dies suddenly, or in a confused or dark state of mind, can become trapped on earth. For example, someone commits suicide and according to their religion they believe they have committed an unforgivable sin that will land them in hell forever. The soul's fear turns into a personal chain that binds them to earth. Or, someone dies while they are extremely depressed; because of a dark mental state, the dead soul does not respond to the light that appears when someone dies—the light of a loved one or a guardian angel, who safely leads the soul into the hereafter. Confused, the depressed soul resists and thus remains stuck on earth.

Prayer can help the dying in another way. In one actual near-death experience, after a car crash, an injured person lay on the ground, dying, their body mangled in great pain. As the person lay there, half dead, they "heard" someone nearby—praying for them. As the stranger prayed, a white light appeared and surrounded the crash victim, removing the extreme pain, until the person was rescued. In another actual experience, a woman in a coma who lay dying in a hospital bed "saw" the prayers of loved ones who stood around her as they prayed for her recovery. Their prayers appeared as rainbow-colored musical notes that vibrated healing at her.

Fear can chain a person to wander the streets as a ghost, until they see the light and follow it into the hereafter; prayer helps to release such chained souls. Whether you say a silent prayer for an accident victim as you pass a car crash or pray for a deceased loved one, never hesitate to pray.

EXAMPLES OF VISITS FROM THE DEAD

When you dream of a loved one who has died, the author often says: Some dreams are not dreams. They are actual visits that you remember as a dream, because a dream is your only vehicle of memory while you sleep. With few distractions during sleep, it is easier for a dead loved one to reconnect, as in these examples of a wide range of visits from those in the hereafter.

Anniversary Visits From Those Who Have Died

Many dream visits take place on the anniversary of someone's death, or on a special day, like a birthday. A dead loved one can also be drawn by your love and make a dream visit simply to reconnect and say hello. Feelings of love and longing can initiate an invisible phone call to a deceased loved one; those who have passed on hear you telepathically, and may respond with a dream visit. A bride-to-be whose father had been her best friend lost her dad a year before she met her husband. A few days before their wedding, the groom received a night-time visit from her dead dad. In the groom's dream, the deceased father-in-law looked the groom in the eye and said, three times: Promise me you will take care of her! The groom promised.

NIGHTMARE

Anniversary Visit, Example #1:
I Am So Sorry

The Dreamer: When his father died after a long illness, nineteen-year-old Arturo felt great sadness; one reason was because he had not been at his father's deathbed. Arturo felt shame, thinking he had not been a good son. Two weeks later, Arturo had a dream.

> He sees his father asleep in bed. Suddenly his father wakes up and looks at him. The word "bangungot" comes to Arturo, which, for a Filipino, denotes a soul that wandered off but is not really dead. Sensing time is short, Arturo expresses sorrow for all he had done

wrong, and for not being there at the end, which his father acknowledges with a warm smile, indicating his love.

As a rare exchange across unknown shores, it was a dream visit Arturo will never forget.

Anniversary Visit, Example #2:
I Miss You So Much

The Dreamer: Eighteen-year-old Ellie and her father were like two peas on a pod. When he died after an unexpected six-month battle with cancer, the shock left Ellie reeling and lonely. She missed her father more than anyone could know. A month later, Ellie had a dream.

Her dad walks through the door, yells her name with happiness, and sits down next to her. Ellie asks her father for a hug, which he gives. She is surprised and scared, yet ecstatic; it feels so real. When Ellie woke up, she remembered that the night before, she had asked her father to make a physical appearance, and promised that she would not be afraid if it happened.

Be careful what you wish for—you may get it.

Anniversary Visit, Example #3:
Love Never Dies

The Dreamer: Twenty-nine-year-old Ida was best friends with her dad and even though she was a single mom with many burdens, she took care of her father through his long illness. When he died, Ida felt a hole in her heart; he was the father that any child would be thrilled to have. Exactly a year after he died, Ida had a dream.

> In the dream, Ida is in the kitchen making something to eat and suddenly sees her dad standing there. She says "It is good to have you back, Daddy," and they hug. Ida can feel him, smell his familiar scent, and feels tears of joy stream down her cheeks. As she experiences his presence during the dream, her logical mind wonders how such a reunion can be happening. However, her heart simply accepts the father–daughter bond that is as strong as ever, and knows it will always be that way.

DREAM VISITS BY THE DEAD— AS COMFORT

Most dream visits by the dearly departed bring comfort and joy. Whether here or in the hereafter, where there is love, a bond can be permanent. Mystics hint that dying is like walking from one room into another. You remain who you are, though souls in the hereafter also grow and learn.

NIGHTMARE

Visits That Comfort, Example #1:
Generations of Love

The Dreamer: Janet was born long after her maternal grandmother had died. Janet loved to leaf through family photo albums and listen to stories about ancestors; her grandmother became a familiar figure who resonated for Janet. Relatives remarked that she and her grandmother were alike in many ways. At twenty-eight, Janet was going through a challenging time; her grandmother made a surprise dream visit.

> Bridging the gap of time and space, the dream grandmother approaches Janet with tears in her eyes and tenderly hugs her. Janet felt comforted and strengthened beyond words, feeling she could handle any challenge, as her grandmother once had.

Talk about ancestral connections! Theirs surpassed those found on Ancestry.com.

NIGHTMARE

Visits That Comfort, Example #2:
You Are Still My Little Girl

The Dreamer: All her life, Celeste addressed her father as Daddy, and he always greeted her as Meha, which is Spanish for daughter. At age sixty-three, Celeste faced challenges that left her feeling devastated and alone. Until . . . she had a visit dream.

> In her dream, Celeste walks into a diner and sees her father sitting in a booth, watching her as she enters. Her heart overflowing with joy, Celeste says "Hi, Daddy," and he says "Hi, Meha," like they always had, and then they exchange a kiss on the cheek. Her father's presence infused Celeste with a comfort and strength that empowered her through a handful of difficulties.

DREAM VISITS BY THE DEAD—
PLUS A MESSAGE

In most dream visits, the deceased is silent—and if words are employed, they tend to be few and transmitted as thoughts, rather than spoken. Dream visits are fairly common; someone in every group has a story to share. However, bridging the gap with a direct communication is an extra, complicated leap from the heavens which few deceased souls achieve. In most cases, the love that radiates from a dead loved one in itself speaks volumes. Nevertheless, once in a while a dream visit does include a message either as direct words or as a visual metaphor that imparts an equivalent meaning.

NIGHTMARE

Visits from the Dead with a Message, Example #1:
Dead Mom Advises Teen

The Dreamer: As a youngster, Stephen felt very lucky to be adopted by a loving family. But at age thirteen, he was devastated when his adoptive mother passed away. By sixteen, he began to have fears that he might lose his dad too. Stephen's intense teenage angst skyrocketed into a series of what-ifs that tied him up in knots—until he received a dream visit from his departed mom.

> The dream began as a family car ride. Stephen, his sister, and his father and mother are singing in the car as they drive to church, having a good time. Stephen loves to sing and is filled with joy that his mother is there, singing with the family. He desperately wants to talk to her; but when he tries to speak, words will not come out. Yet Stephen feels encompassed by her love, and that is enough. Stephen woke up feeling healed and uplifted.

Analysis: As a metaphor, singing held the message "Do what you love, develop your talents, be yourself." The destination, a church, was also indirect advice from his mother as a metaphor that said "Keep a spiritual direction and you will find your way." Holding his mother's love close to his heart, a renewed Stephen went forward without fear.

Visits from the Dead with a Message, Example #2:
A Date Gone Wrong

The Dreamer: Fourteen months after the sudden death of her fiancé, fifty-six-year-old Pamela still felt a mixture of love, anger, and frustration at his passing. They were together for nine years; he was the love of her life. However, the fiancé had never put his financial affairs in order, so his sudden death left Pamela in a financial mess, one that left Pam wondering if he had really loved her.

> In a dream visit, her beau answers the question. He rides up to her on a motorcycle, looking like a young stud, and invites Pam to lunch. She hops up behind him on the bike. They ride to a well-known mountain-top restaurant where they have never dined but had always wanted to. When they arrive, the restaurant is closed. It has closed at two o'clock; it is now three. Knowing they cannot share a meal, Pam and her beau agree they will arrive earlier the next time.

Analysis: Pam woke up shocked, harboring bittersweet feelings of love for him, tinged with the disappointment of saying goodbye all over again. However, she realized they had parted in peace and understanding. Pam understood that the failed restaurant date was an indirect apology from her dead fiancé that said: "I love you, and if I could do it over again I would do it differently." Reassured, Pam's anger vanished. She would always love him, but it was time to move on.

Visits from the Dead with a Message, Example #3:
A Mother's Blessing

The Dreamer: When the company where Zach had worked for many years downsized, Zach was laid off. He trembled; it would be difficult to find a new job at fifty-seven; experience was no longer an automatic plus. As the two-year anniversary of the death of his mother approached, his mother visited her anxious son in a dream. The mother-son duo had been best friends who loved to share a meal.

> In the dream, she tells Zach she is fine, then helps him pack for a business trip. As a metaphor about "being on one's way," packing suggested that she knew Zach was looking for work. His mother says to Zach: "You will be fine, all will work out, though your table is not yet ready." Stunned, Zach woke up energized, her presence felt so real.

Analysis: The dream reminded him of the regular dinner reservations he and his mom used to share. They loved to relax at the bar of a restaurant with a glass of wine until their dinner table was ready. His mother's words that he had a reservation, even though the table was not ready, told Zach what he wanted—a decent new job—was in his future. Comforted, Zach brought a new confidence to job interviews, and, as his mom predicted, it all worked out.

DREAM VISITS BY THE DEAD— WITH AN ANNOUNCEMENT OF DEATH

Sometimes in a dream visit by someone who is dead, the deceased suggests that someone who is alive is getting ready to join them. Such announcements are meant to help prepare the person and their loved ones for the transition and suggest that the impending death is meant to be.

Visits with a Death Announcement, Example #1:
Dead Dad in Search of Someone

The Dreamer: Fifty-year-old Molly had a dream about her dead father, with whom she had been close; her deceased brother was also in the dream.

> In the dream, Molly is at a funeral, standing beside her mother, who was still alive in real life. Molly is surprised at her mother's appearance; her elderly mother looks young and gorgeous, as she had when she was young. A young man in a white sports jacket is nearby, wearing a jacket that Molly's dead brother used to wear. Suddenly Molly sees her father, who had died ten years earlier, standing at the door as if he has just arrived. Excited, Molly screams: "Oh, my God, there's Daddy!!!" But instead of responding, her father frantically looks around as if searching and waiting for someone. In her excitement, Molly wants to hug her father, but as she moves toward him, she wakes up.

Analysis: Those who die often appear in a dream as they had been in their prime. Molly's elderly mother was still alive in real life, yet in the dream she looks youthful and pristine, like a young bride. Her mother's appearance and the frantic seeking that Molly's father displays say it all. The scene of Molly's dad waiting for her mother to join him, together with the opening scene of the funeral, confirms the announcement as the reason for the visit. The dream visit by Molly's father is a metaphoric announcement that her mother's soul is preparing to move on.

Molly said: "I woke up crying, I was so excited to see my dad. Yet somehow I felt he was there for my mom. She looked so perfect, so untouched, so unreal. I am at peace with that. It made sense that my brother was there. He was a mama's boy, and, dead or alive, he would attend my mother's funeral and would be waiting for her arrival in the afterlife, along with my dad."

Visits with a Death Announcement, Example #2:
Happy Trails to You, Until We Meet Again . . .

The Dreamer: Fifty-six-year-old Sergio was young at heart and maintained close family ties across several generations. In his Latino heritage, family was the foundation of life's joy. Mystic threads like having dreams about the dead, did not scare Sergio.

> In Sergio's dream, his deceased grandfather stands in a doorway, looking younger and impeccably dressed as he always did. Sergio calls out; his grandfather waves and smiles. Another door opens and Sergio's mother, who was still alive, walks in. She looks radiant; she is all dressed up and has a fancy hairdo. His grandfather takes Sergio's mother by the hand and they walk out together.

Said Sergio: "It felt awesome, like he was trying to tell me that my ninety-one-year-old mom was going to pass on."

Dream Analsis: That sounds right. Sergio's mom was glowing, which suggests a happy transition. We grieve; but for those who lived a decent life, dying is a positive event as the soul returns to a heavenly home and reunites with loved ones, in eternity.

A VISIT FROM A DEAD PERSON
WHO NEEDS PRAYER

Though only God knows if and how often it may happen, because the possibility is rare—once in a blue moon, a soul who dies, either suddenly or in a state of fear or depression, may get stuck on Earth. Like the dead guys portrayed in the movie Ghost, such wandering souls need prayers to get back on track and follow the light of an angel or loved one who shows up when you die, to lead you into the hereafter. If that sounds like fiction, read up on near-death experiences (NDEs) and decide for yourself.

`NIGHTMARE`

Visits from the Dead Who Need Prayer, Example #1:
Not Yet Recovered

The Dreamer: Twenty-nine-year-old Sandra lost her beloved father ten days after her wedding day. She grieved deeply. He had been ill for several years, but that did not cushion the pain of his loss.

> Four months later, Sandra saw her dad in a dream, sitting in a chair in her home. It felt so real that Sandra wondered if her father was still alive, and it was wonderful to see him. However, when Sandra woke up, she felt troubled. Her father seemed as sick and as weak in the dream as he had been during his long illness.

Analysis: In most dream visits, the deceased looks normal or even better than they did when alive. Sandra's unsettled feelings were a clue, along with her father's weak appearance, as hints that he needed her prayers. In the final analysis only God knows what is true; yet praying for her dad could only help, which is what Sandra chose to do.

Visits from the Dead Who Need Prayer, Example #2:
Mother, I Am Here

The Dreamer: Fifty-two-year-old Naomi grieved intensely at the sudden death of her thirty-one-year-old son.

> As her broken heart stumbled through the days, a few weeks later Naomi began to have a recurring dream of her son standing in her home. In the dream, no words are spoken; she and her son simply walk from his room into the kitchen. The dreams puzzled Naomi. They also scared her.

What the Dream Analyst Said to the Dreamer: "Most dream visits from the deceased are messages to let tell you they still love you and live on in the afterlife. However, your son died a sudden death. There is a possibility that at the moment of his death, he felt confused and became stuck and stayed close to what was familiar, namely, you and your home. He clung to you instead of following the light of an angel into eternity. You are the one he knows and trusts. Though only God knows for sure—if that were the case, your son needs prayer to help him find his way. Church groups often place the name of a deceased loved one onto a prayer list; add your son's name. Pray for your son and trust that, with your love, he will find his way into the hereafter and will be at peace. Keep in mind that peace is what he wants for you, too, despite the painful loss. As you give him a gift of peace through prayer, let that peace also fill your heart."

BONUS TRACK—EXAMPLES OF VISITS
FROM PETS WHO HAVE DIED

After the loss of a beloved pet, many wonder if the pet will greet them in the afterlife. Some, including the author, have had dream visits from a deceased pet. For many, pets are like family members, so it makes sense that a pet would make a dream visit to let you know they still love you and assure you that they are well, somewhere in eternity. When there is a heart connection, as you are grieving for a pet or animal friend, watch for a dream. Or, better still . . . ask for a dream visit. In mystic dream connections, all is possible.

NIGHTMARE

Visits with a Dead Pet, Example #1:
Snoozing Among the Shrubs

The Dreamer: Forty-eight-year-old Gabe had a black kitty named Buster; Gabe and Buster shared several homes during their fifteen happy years together. When Buster died, grief seared Gabe's tender heart; a dream eased his pain.

> As the dream begins, Gabe is in his backyard, looking for Buster. Others nearby tell Gabe it will be impossible to find his cat because the pet was lost in a forest and could be anywhere. But with the instinct of total love, Gabe walks straight to a green shrub; there, nestled inside, snoozed his pet. Buster looks up, thrilled to see Gabe. Gabe takes Buster in his arms; the kitty is very happy to be reunited with him.

When alive, Buster had loved to snooze inside a garden shrub. In the dream, Gabe feels the undying love they had shared, and knows his beloved Buster had found a comfortable, safe resting place in the great beyond.

Visits with a Dead Pet, Example #2:
Playing Happily in Still Water

The Dreamer: Viola loved her orange tabby, Homer; the cat's peaceful nature calmed her after a stressful day at work. When Homer became ill and reached death's door, Viola summoned a vet to her home; the vet ended Homer's suffering. As the beloved cat died peacefully in Viola's arms, a quiet grief settled in.

> Weeks later, Viola had a dream: her orange tabby is sitting in the middle of a shallow pond, taking everything in, just as Homer used to do in her backyard pond. The water in the dream pond is very still. Homer bats his paw to stir the water, which the cat loved to do when alive. Viola sees that her pet is happy, and that Homer is where he needs to be. Amused, Viola notes that her pet is its old self, but now has a larger pond to play in.

Analysis: American clairvoyant Edgar Cayce gave readings on many topics; he suggested that when pets are loved, they can retain their spirit essence and accompany a human friend through several lifetimes. Embracing her mystic side, Viola held that thought; she and Homer had a bond which felt eternal.

Visits with a Dead Pet, Example #3:
Staircase to Heaven

The Dreamer: Bill loved his chocolate Lab, Charlie; when his canine companion died after a sudden and quick illness, Bill was inconsolable.

Unable to shake his grief, Bill dreams that he is standing at the bottom of a staircase that goes all the way up to heaven; and to his delight, Charlie is right beside him. Bill begins to climb the stairs; Charlie follows. Bill reaches a middle rung and can climb no farther, but Charlie continues to climb. Bill calls out, but Charlie doesn't come back; Bill knows his pet can no longer follow him.

Analysis: The dream visit felt real. Bill could feel Charlie's deep love for him, a love that unchained Bill's sorrow. Like the words of a song about a staircase to heaven, Bill accepted that his pet was happy in the hereafter.

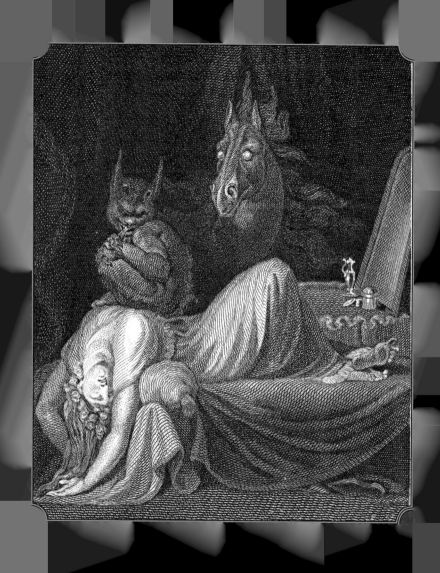

CHAPTER EIGHT

Super-Intense Nightmares

Not all nightmares are created equal. Regular nightmares are scary enough, but in addition, there are super-scary nightmares such as the recurring bad dreams which appear after a trauma such as experiencing the loss of a home due to fire or flood; the nightmares of sensitive people; and scary dream experiences of people who are in the throes of an extreme life challenge. When life turns up the heat and feelings get intense, a handful of super-intense nightmares may follow.

In the prism of nightmares that people can experience, three nightmare types fall outside the norm. Examples of such beyond-the-norm nightmares follow.

* *Nightmares and PTSD.* Many experience nightmares after a specific trauma or disaster such as war, flood or hurricane, mass murder, terrorist attack, incest, rape, and sexual assault. Traumatic nightmares replay the painful event over and over again and can persist for months or even years. Nightmares that begin after a trauma can be a symptom of Post-Traumatic Stress Disorder (PTSD), a psychological condition that can disrupt the person's emotions and mental functioning. Some, diagnosed with PTSD, also experience a breakdown in normal sleep and dream patterns, which, along with the nightmares, creates a degree of exhaustion and depression that hinders them from leading a normal life.

* *Nightmares of the Tender-Hearted.* Those of a more delicate constitution can have unique nightmares. Like having no sunscreen for protection, the emotionally thin-skinned tend to experience more pain, which leads to more nightmares than most people encounter.

* *Nightmares during an Extreme Life Challenge.* Last but not least, life itself can become a living nightmare for some. Their nightmares mirror the terror of being in a situation that seems to have no way out.

NIGHTMARES AND PTSD

Recurring nightmares that begin after a specific trauma and persist for more than a month are different than regular nightmares. They can exhibit some or all of the following features.

Scenes Replayed, Over and Over Again. As a side effect of a traumatic experience, nightmares may replay the pain and horror a person had during a terrifying incident or disaster.

Scenes Are Severe and Intense. Because scenes replay an actual trauma, the nightmares feel severe. Think about the most terrifying experience in your life and imagine what it would be like to relive that event every night. Yet what feels traumatic varies from person to person; feelings and reactions are subjective and hard to describe. What scares one person may not scare another, yet each may have intense, painful nightmares after an event that feels traumatic.

A Broken REM Cycle. When nightmares happen after a traumatic event, for some the sleep–dream cycle can become disrupted. Sleep and dream phases (known as Rapid Eye Movement or REM phases) may not function correctly. Normal sleep has a 90-minute cycle which starts as a light sleep (Stage 1), proceeds to a deeper sleep (Stage 2) where eye movement and muscle activity stop, then goes into sleep's deepest level (Stage 3). Someone who is awakened during Stage 3 can feel disoriented. After spending a few minutes in deep sleep, you cycle back up through Stages 2 and 1, back into a light sleep. Some call the "going back up" steps Stages 4 and 5 of sleep and dreaming. Whatever the labels, the end result is a circular, 90-minute round trip of sleep (from light to deep, and back up again to light).

A special event takes place at the end of this 90-minute sleep cycle: you dream. Most people experience three or four 90-minute cycles of sleep per night. However, that is not true for a traumatized person with a disrupted sleep cycle. Like an antenna that has become too sensitive, a traumatized person's fear or anxiety wakes them up before they get through a full 90-minute cycle, and, as a result, they lose the recuperative benefits of sleep. A normal person can go to bed troubled, yet wake up feeling better. Trauma victims with a disrupted sleep cycle wake up feeling just as bad as—or worse—than they did when they went to sleep. To cope with unbearable physical and emotional exhaustion, some trauma victims use alcohol or drugs, which compounds their troubles. If you notice someone who has experienced a trauma, cannot sleep, and has intense nightmares, try to steer them toward a therapist.

How a Black Teen Was Traumatized and Acquired a Lifetime of Extreme Nightmares

This is a first-hand account, given to the author by a black combat veteran diagnosed with post-traumatic stress. Anthony's story is a revealing glimpse into how and why traumatic nightmares happen. Events took place during the Vietnam War era, events that plunged this nineteen-year-old into a lifetime of nightmares. Told in his own words, Anthony's story is also the story of many combat veterans—then, and now.

" . . . This is how I got into the Army. It was 1968. I was eighteen; there was a lot of racism in Virginia where I lived and we were fighting for freedom. One time, twenty buses were leaving from Norfolk to Alabama, to march with Martin Luther King. About halfway to Alabama, a crowd of angry white men, who knew we were coming, barricaded the highway. They shouted at us, threw rocks, and started shooting at our buses. We could not go forward, so the buses turned back. We were angry. When we got back to Richmond, Virginia, we heard on the radio that Martin Luther King had just been assassinated. Our anger turned to rage. We streamed out of the buses, threw rocks, and broke store windows.

"The police caught me and immediately brought me before a judge, in night court. The judge gave me an ultimatum: I could spend two years in jail or do two years service in the Army. I asked if I would have to go into battle. The Vietnam war was going on and I did not want to go into the jungles and fight. He asked if I could read and write; I said yes. He asked if I could type; I said yes. He said because I knew how to type, I would be assigned to a supply unit. So I agreed to enlist, and the next morning I signed up for the Army.

"After a few months of training, instead of being assigned to an office supply unit like I was told would happen, I was shipped out to fight with an all-white Army unit. The unit commanders gave me jobs like burning manure and fixing tires, the worst jobs there were. One day I asked why they had not given me the job I'd been trained to do, as a supply clerk; they did not like that I asked questions. The next day the sergeant held out two pieces of paper in front of me, and told me to pick one. He said that whichever one I picked, that was where they were going to send me the next day. I refused. So he picked one and read a paper that said: Infantry lines. I think he was messing with me: both papers probably said the same thing.

"The next morning I was shipped right into the middle of a battle zone where fighting was in progress. As soon as my plane landed, I had to scramble into a helicopter that was going into a battle zone. I took my machine gun and jumped on. A few minutes later, we approached a landing field near a battle zone, and as we got close, the helicopter got hit. I did not know what to do. I was terrified, and though we were still in the air, I jumped out. Seconds later, the helicopter blew up while I was still in midair. The other nine guys got killed. I was so scared when I hit the ground that I came up shooting, until I heard someone shout that I was not in a combat zone.

"The next day I was assigned to keep watch at night. I fell asleep, I was not used to staying up all night. I don't know what woke me up; I did not hear a sound. A Viet Cong was standing beside me, ready to cut my throat, but I shot him. The other guys had fallen asleep, too; their throats were cut. One thing after another like that kept happening. It affected me so much. The terror stayed with me. It took me seventeen years to cry. As a teenager, I was gentle and soft-mouthed. As a combat soldier, I withdrew into myself. I resented authority. It felt like the military was trying to kill me, to murder me and my people."

Trauma and Emotions—Feelings Engraved in the Unconscious

A trauma ends, but the reactions to the trauma can become deeply engraved in an unconscious part of your mind, and such fear-etched emotions are not easy to unplug. As the author discovered while writing two master's theses at the College of William and Mary about PTSD and nightmares—when feelings linked to a trauma imprint themselves into the unconscious, the embedded emotions can act almost as a form of hypnosis—a self-hypnosis "side effect" that is very hard to reverse. That is why cognitive therapies for trauma victims that focus only on discussing the trauma, like a thought Band-aid, do not tend to erase the vivid images and deeply embedded emotional scars.

In an earlier chapter, the author claimed that all dreams have a helpful purpose and some research suggests that one purpose of dreaming is to digest painful feelings. Nightmares after a trauma replay the painful events, and like waves against rough rocks, over time the replayed scenes can smooth out an emotional scar. One sign of healing is that the instant-replay images begin to include normal, everyday items that are not related to the trauma. As scenes become more general and less specific to the original event, traumatic memories may subside, and, in time, disappear. To get a feel for what it is like to have traumatic nightmares, read through the following examples.

TRAUMA AND NIGHTMARES—
IN COMBAT VETERANS WITH PTSD

The locations of war can vary, weapons can vary, but the scenes of bloodshed, horror, and terror are the same, as in these firsthand accounts of nightmares of veterans with PTSD that were shared directly with the author.

Example 1:

"I am in the middle of a bridge when the shooting starts. There are rockets and automatic weapons. Men are falling everywhere as they run for cover. Most are returning fire, it seems like the firing will never stop. Men are making sounds of death. I look for Sarge but cannot find him. I run into the woods and take cover. I see Sarge, dead, and wake up, terrified."

Example 2:

"Me and my Marine buddies are on patrol, walking down a narrow path. We receive incoming fire from the enemy. We retreat. The road is booby-trapped with explosives and five guys are wounded. They scream to God for help, I am scared to death. I wake up, my shirt and pillow are soaked with sweat."

Example 3:

"We are walking through a jungle, using machetes to make a path. It is unbearably hot, I am exhausted, vines keep pulling me back, and bugs are biting. All of a sudden all hell breaks loose, guys are hollering and screaming—we've walked into an ambush. Jesus, I'm so scared, but I fire my machine gun. The enemy is running, I am trying to hit them. My gun jams, oh shit, not now. I tell the guy next to me I need more ammo, he does not move, so I grab his arm. He is dead. I wake up in terror."

Example 4:

"I am back in Vietnam, destroying a village. I see their eyes and run. I run and run, seeing only dead faces. I am paralyzed with horror."

Example 5:

"We're on patrol and a firefight breaks out. I look down and see red, dark red, then the body of a man that I've killed. I run away at great speed. Terrified, I woke up. I was sitting in a chair beside my bed, holding my shoe. I thought it was my .45 caliber. Books and clothes were strewn all around. I did not know how they got there."

Example 6:

"I'm in a foxhole, gas is all around me. I see people falling beside me shouting 'Help me,' but by the time I get to them it's too late. There are body bags all over the place. I say to myself 'Not again, why do people always die around me.' It was awful."

Example 7:

"I'm in a boat, traveling up the river in Vietnam. We take on sniper fire, my M-16 is not working and the .50 cal will not do the job. I watch a friend take a round, there's blood, deep red blood, everywhere. As I woke up, I hit the bedroom wall and wanted to kill or blow something up. My bed was torn apart. This mission actually happened."

TRAUMA AND NIGHTMARES—
IN THE GENERAL POPULATION

Whatever the original incident, those who have persistent, severe nightmares need understanding and support.

Trauma and Nightmares, Example #1:
Stalked by My Dead Father

The Dreamer: About three times a week, which is a lot, forty-three-year-old Zara had a nightmare about her dead father.

> In her dreams, Zara sees her father in strange places like a train, a hospital waiting room, or standing near a window. She knows that her father is dead, and tells him so. Her father always smiles and appears happy. However, in real life, her father had molested Zara as a child, exposed himself in her face, and never apologized for his actions—even on his deathbed. To Zara, these repeated scenes of meeting her father were intensely disturbing.

Analysis: The nightmares told a story about encounters with someone who appears to enjoy themselves, even though the other person is anxious and troubled. The scenes echoed what Zara experienced as a child as scars she still carried; Zara had not healed from the trauma of being molested. And though her father was at fault, Zara retained a child-like anger and shame. As a continued knock on the door, nightmares asked Zara to take steps to heal those feelings. Zara and others like her can and do find a path to healing. An incest-survivors group and a therapist who specializes in healing the wounds of child molesters can be a great help.

Trauma and Nightmares, Example #2:
Dead Father Turns His Back on Me

The Dreamer: Natalie's parents were divorced. Because her father suffered from depression, Natalie was raised by a single mom. Natalie hardly ever saw her father, and she barely knew him. Nevertheless, a child often holds a fantasy version of a missing parent and remains emotionally attached to the fantasy version, even if the parent is absent or emotionally distant.

Despite her father's history with depression, Natalie and her mother were shocked when he shot himself. By then, Natalie was a young adult in her early twenties. While her father was alive, Natalie never dreamed about him; after he died, she had a recurring dream about him that filled her with horror.

> In the nightmare, Natalie sees her father and tries to talk to him. But each time they meet, her father turns and walks away, leaving Natalie confused and in anguish. Natalie was losing sleep; her concerned mother consulted a dream analyst.

Analysis: The sudden death of Natalie's father had opened a deep, hidden wound. Though she never knew her father as a child, Natalie longed for a father's paternal love and held a fantasy version of him in her heart; when he died, Natalie lost the chance to reach out. Emotionally, both the real father and the fantasy dad had died, for Natalie. And a parent who commits suicide throws a new emotional time bomb at a child—a time bomb Natalie needed to get defused. Children can unconsciously identify with the emotional patterns of a parent; the father's suicide was a powerful hidden, unconscious message that rocked Natalie's world, saying "Am I emotionally weak, like my father? Could I fall apart, like he did?"

As the author learned in a seminar led by suicide survivors who shared their stories, suicide is not about depression: *Suicide is about pain.* A person who tries to take their own life is attempting to stop an unbearable pain. Sadly, statistics suggest that when a parent commits suicide, it can raise the odds that a child may do the same, later in their lives.

The nightmares that began after her father's death brought Natalie face-to-face with deep levels of pain that she had been hiding from herself all of her life. Her father's death triggered a trauma that Natalie could not put into words—the pain of missing a father, and unconscious feelings of rejection because of his absence. To a child, the reason a parent is absent does not matter: the child simply feels pain. However, once named, wounds can heal. As Natalie and others discover, working with a therapist can heal any wound, which, in time, restores happiness.

THE UNIQUE NIGHTMARES OF SENSITIVE, CREATIVE, AND ARTISTIC INDIVIDUALS

For most people, nightmares are about personal issues that generate fear and anxiety. Those who are intensely sensitive can experience nightmares for a different reason. Emotions of those who are sensitive or high-strung can act like a mega-antenna that tunes in to the pain and suffering of others that bubbles around them.

There are benefits to being super-sensitive. Creative people—whether artists, engineers, or problem solvers in any field—often see life through a colorful kaleidoscope that brings amazing and unique perspectives. Their unusual antennas perform a high-wire act that brings success and satisfaction; it can also leave those who are sensitive in emotional tatters. Sensitivity can be like overeating: you get an upset tummy—and nightmares.

Ordinary people with marshmallow hearts can also have super-size emotional antennae. At a dream seminar, forty-year-old Andy wondered why he had constant nightmares: his dreams featured people with bloody faces, shootings, and violence. Andy led a normal life and enjoyed his work as a bus driver. Digging deeper, Andy realized he was unconsciously tuning in to the suffering that he saw on the faces of his passengers. Andy's tender heart soaked up their pain like a sponge, which brought on nightmares. Someone at the seminar suggested that Andy start each day by surrounding passengers with God's perfect love, to heal and strengthen them and himself. Sounds like a plan . . . whatever works!

Take a look at the following three examples of nightmares experienced by the highly sensitive:

`NIGHTMARE`

Nightmares and Sensitivity, Example #1:
Rage beneath Still Waters

The Dreamer: Bridget was a talented artist. Though raised in a wealthy family, she worked hard in art school to improve her craft. Bridget was puzzled by the constant nightmares she had experienced since childhood.

> Her daily dreams were filled with blood-curdling violence, death, and rampaging killers. Bridget often woke up petrified, dripping with sweat.

Analysis: The scary dreams did not jive with Bridget's placid personality. By day, she was the soul of calm and reason, but as a wild artiste, Bridget adorned art canvases with bold colors and vivid, dramatic scenes.

After a few rounds of self-exploration, Bridget noted two sides to her personality: she had a calm side that loved a quiet, normal life; she also had an intense, passionate side, hidden deep in a secret chamber—a wild woman who made her presence felt through Bridget's art. Somewhere along the road to growing up, Bridget developed a coping strategy for the two sides of her personality. She channeled her calm, practical side into a normal daily routine. And to her secret delight, Bridget let her explosive, passionate, and creative side rip into dramatic, colorful art pieces. Bridget instinctively channeled her seesaw of emotions into a wholesome life. Talk about a yin/yang harmony. You go, girl!

NIGHTMARE

Nightmares and Sensitivity, Example #2:
Teen Chased by Dinosaur

The Dreamer: An occasional dream about being chased can mirror vulnerable feelings about a specific issue. But when intense, recurring nightmares about being chased persist, it can flag a highly sensitive personality. That was true for seventeen-year-old Pete.

> Pete's recurring nightmares about being chased through a jungle by a T. Rex dinosaur featured blood-curdling roars, a life-and-death version of a game of hide-and-go-seek, and being constantly hunted, for unknown reasons.

Analysis: Life at age seventeen can feel vulnerable for any teen; some, like Pete, register at the extreme upper end of the sensitivity scale. Most teens develop a thicker skin as they mature; some, like Pete, need an extra oak tree or two, under which to shelter for a while, until they find and express their unique strengths. Why are some people more sensitive than others? What made Pete feel vulnerable and afraid? Though he had issues to work out, the reasons may not matter. Instead, keep an eye out for thin-skinned folks of any age. If they are not stomped upon, the sensitive among us can sprinkle much needed rainbow and fairy dust onto a humdrum society.

Nightmares and Sensitivity, Example #3:
Teen Sees an Endangered Llama

The Dreamer: By age eighteen, Lily had frequent nightmares about animals in distress.

> A recurring nightmare featured a lovely white llama, running in terror down a busy highway. Lily tries to save the llama, but all she can do is watch as cars swerve to avoid hitting the desperate creature. Finally, a group of boys grabs the llama. But instead of rescuing the vulnerable animal, they harass it; they are mean and cruel. As the dream ends, Lily sees a closeup of the creature's petrified face, and she wakes up in agony.

Analysis: Dreams often mirror the window through which you experience life, at least at that time. Frequent dreams about suffering animals can signal a dreamer's heightened sensitivity. The recurring nightmare told a story about trying to save a gentle, special creature that was vulnerable and out of place. Like the llama, Lily was a tender, unique teenager who often felt out of place among her more aggressive schoolmates. Like the endangered llama, Lily often felt under siege by the mean words of bullies and the violence she saw in the world around her. Lily experienced life as a gentle llama, stuck on the highway of life that sometimes felt overwhelming and threatening. There is merit in toughening up and developing coping skills, which most teens eventually accomplish. There is also a lot to be said for preserving the world's unique, rare llamas and tender orchids—the sensitive teens and adults like Lily.

DREAMS DURING EXTREME LIFE CHALLENGES: WHEN LIFE IS A LIVING NIGHTMARE

Most challenges, large or small, are like a speed bump: whether they are difficult or simply annoying, you get past them. But sooner or later you may meet a brick wall as an obstacle so enormous that it feels like you cannot get past it. A young man may face the loss of a limb. A sweetheart loses a fiancé. A family, devastated by a flood or hurricane, loses everything. In countries at war, many become refugees without a home or country. A man endures a prison sentence for a crime he did not commit. Whatever the extreme and often unexpected event, in an instant—all is lost. Life has become a living nightmare.

Some call times of overwhelming challenge the Dark Night of the Soul. Modern mystic Eckhart Tolle describes the Dark Night of the Soul as a time when nothing makes sense anymore; all that you believed no longer seems valid. The framework of your life collapses, and you feel disconnected and powerless. Nightmares capture the pain, horror, and desolation of the dark night of the soul.

Dream messages never have all the answers, but they can be a safe harbor to anchor the mind and feelings as you seek a way out during a storm. When you suffer, dreams translate your dark, empty feelings into scenes of turbulent storms, climbing steep mountains, rising flood waters, drifting on the ocean, and being stuck in strange places. During a turbulent time, a dream message can shine a ray of hope or let you peek around the corner as a glimpse into the end of your travail.

When stuck on an emotional cliff with nothing to hold on to, a dream can play a song of heavenly beauty that uplifts, and for a brief second you feel whole again. Such tender whispers help you find your way back. Like an invisible dear companion, the psyche offers tiny morsels that heal, and over time reconnect you to the strength and talents you need to rebuild your life. Been there. Done that. So have countless others. Both "Bankrupt and Penniless" and "A Victim of

Financial Scam" on the following pages describe nightmares that occur during the dark night of the soul.

Nightmares During an Extreme Life Challenge, Example #1:
Bankrupt and Penniless

The Dreamer: Patricia was a fifty-five-year-old single woman with a modest income; she had no family to lean on. When her small business venture went bankrupt, she was shocked to find herself jobless and penniless. It was a time of economic hardship for many; companies were not hiring. On the verge of losing her home and with few prospects, Patricia froze, imagining a future as a homeless bag lady. Nightmares echoed her fears, yet also showed the way forward.

Soldier On

In one nightmare, a soldier is on night maneuvers. Bombs explode all around him, and the road is so dark that the soldier cannot see the trail. Though terrified, he pushes forward, on and on; it feels like forever. Finally, the soldier sees a marker in the distance that signals the end of the trail. He still has a long way to go but feels relieved; the end is in sight, he can make it.

Analysis: Patricia was the terrified soldier groping in the dark as she tried to find a job and build a new life. The end of a dream often points the way forward. In Patricia's dream, the end was in sight; she just had to keep trying. For the first time in months, Patricia woke up feeling hopeful that if she persisted, she would find a job and land on her feet.

Steep Mountain Climb

Months passed and Patricia was still jobless. Hope vanished and her feelings crashed, a downward dip that was captured in a nightmare about climbing a mountain during a blizzard.

> In the nightmare, Patricia treks down a long mountain road in the snow, a road packed with refugees escaping from a war-torn country. The mountain is so steep, it is almost vertical. Yet it's the only way forward, so the weary travelers march on. The long, grueling road goes on forever with no end in sight. Suddenly, Patricia is shocked. In an instant she finds herself at the top of the mountain, crossing a small ridge. On the other side of the mountain, she sees a paved road with an easy downward slope. The snow is gone; the sky is blue and sunny. Patricia has reached a turning point where everything is beautiful and easy. She woke up, elated.

Analysis: There was hope. However, the nightmare hinted getting there would take patience, perseverance, and fortitude. Yes. It happened. In time, Patricia found a job that was just right and began a new life that was better than ever.

NIGHTMARE

Nightmares During an Extreme Life Challenge, Example #2:
A Victim of Financial Scam

The dreams that Judd experienced have also occurred during the dark night of the Soul.

The Dreamer: At age fifty-eight, Judd lost most of his life earnings in a financial scam that also demolished others. With only a few career years left to replenish his bank account, Judd was overwhelmed with fear. Shocked, confused, and demoralized at the evil that had befallen him, all Judd could do was sit on his living room sofa for days at a time. Dreams helped Judd take stock, take a breath, and begin to move forward.

Surrounded By the Light

In one of Judd's dreams, a kind older woman tells him that her husband is in the same situation. She advises Judd to surround himself with light before falling asleep.

Analysis: The image of surrounding himself with light resonated for Judd. His mom was a Quaker, a religious community with few formal worship rituals; Quakers often speak of prayer as "surrounding with light." Judd took the dream as a hint to pray at bedtime, and as he prayed nightly, Judd began to feel less vulnerable.

Judd was extremely angry at the manipulators who built their wealth by taking a sledgehammer to the backs of hard-working people like himself. Judd's rage brewed into a constant mental uproar, and even though his anger was justified, as a side effect the mental turmoil clouded his judgment. Judd's scattered thoughts left him befuddled and unable to focus; he needed a cool, calm, and clear head to deal with lawyers and a stack of paperwork. Faced with uncertainty, heavy losses, and overwhelming odds, Judd could not find a calm space inside himself. Until . . . a nightmare came to Judd's rescue.

How to Win a Battle with Evil

In Judd's nightmare, he and a group of strangers are marching through a severe snowstorm in Antarctica, the coldest and most desolate place on earth. Their mission is to connect with another group, take action, then quickly get out of there and return home. However, they have an enemy in their midst, a large man with devil-like features who is intent on stopping them. Known as the evil one, the enemy cuts the group off from its leaders to weaken them. But the group keeps pushing on through the dangerous terrain. Exhausted, many scatter and fall by the side of the road, which makes the group even more vulnerable.

A strong young man in the group emerges as a new leader. Wanting to destroy the group, the evil one challenges the young man to a fight—to the death. The young man accepts the challenge; he is pure of heart and smart, and, though inexperienced, the young man has a strong, impassioned desire to save the group. The fight begins. As they fight, the evil one taunts the young man. The young man takes the bait, becomes incensed at the taunts, and reacts in anger. The evil one gloats; the young man's anger makes him an easier target, which is what the evil one wants.

A wise old woman is watching the fight from the sidelines. She calls out to the young man with sage advice, saying "This is how you deal with evil. Stay calm, do not get angry, stay strong in love and in truth." Thanks to her words, the young man understands that controlling his emotions is the key to winning. Just as the young man realizes what he has to do, Judd wakes up, feeling enormously loved and strong, as if jolted by a lightning bolt of joy.

Analysis: Judd still had insurmountable odds to face, but the dream has infused him with confidence. He took the message to heart: to succeed, rein in your frustration and anger. As Judd applied the old woman's wisdom one day at a time, he began to piece his life back together—with serenity.

DRUG ADDICTION
AS A LIVING NIGHTMARE

Mystics often cite the close connection between the mind and the body: what you think, and what you feel, affects your body. And vice versa: what you eat and ingest affects your mind and feelings. In an electronic age that craves the balance of human warmth, drug addiction illustrates the harsh, overpowering, negative side of this mind–body loop. Nightmares mirror the overwhelming issues that we wrestle with—including addiction, in all its forms. "Billy's Story" and "Amber's Story" that follow, both describe nightmares about drug addiction.

NIGHTMARE

Drug Addiction as an Extreme Life Challenge, Example #1:
Billy's Story

The Dreamer: As a twenty-three-year-old homeless addict who suffered from post-traumatic stress (PTSD), Billy felt scared, alone, and betrayed.

> In a nightmare, Billy is visiting his mother. His younger brother is there, along with a friend. The friend keeps giving Billy dirty looks. Billy and the unknown friend end up alone in a room; the friend pulls a knife and attacks Billy. There is a scuffle; the attacker slashes Billy on the back of the head. Billy manages to restrain the attacker by pushing him against a window; the window breaks and the attacker falls through and dies. Suddenly Billy is back in the main room with his brother, who calls him horrible names and disowns him for what he's done to his friend. Billy explains it was self-defense, but the brother does not care.

Analysis: The story describes how someone tries to explain the bad outcome of a battle that they did not pick, yet loved ones are deaf to explanations and push them away. The story mirrors an addict's predicament: An addict is in a life-and-death battle with drugs and is just trying to survive, yet meets a lack of understanding from those who mean the most to them.

The dream showed that Billy wanted family and others to understand what he was going through; yet, when he tried to explain, arguments happened that made him feel that they did not want to know and did not care. No matter what we go through, we all need to feel loved. Billy had to find the support he needed to find his way back in other ways, like spending time at community centers and clinics. In the dream, he defended himself and prevailed, which showed courage and a desire to get back on his feet. Billy needed to be reminded of his unique talents and strengths, such as a flair for cooking; using and developing such talents would help him turn things around.

`NIGHTMARE`

Drug Addiction as an Extreme Life Challenge, Example #2:
Amber's Story

The Dreamer: As a twenty-nine-year-old addict, Amber felt panic, despair, and worry about the future. Amber has a series of nightmares about being chased.

Chased

In the first nightmare, Amber is chased by a strange man. She locks herself in a bedroom, but the man stands, threatening, on the other side of the door. Amber tells herself he is not a bad guy, the man is merely something else, like an animal. However, as the door bursts open, she wakes up in terror and screams her husband's name.

Analysis: The creature chasing Amber is a metaphor for temptations to use drugs, temptations always at her door, that make her feel extremely vulnerable.

Death of Husband

Amber goes back to sleep and finds herself in a parking lot; her husband is nearby. As she drives away, a gunman shoots. Gang members block the exits and kill everyone who is trapped inside the parking lot. Amber escapes, but worries about her husband; when she calls him, gang members answer his phone; on her phone video, Amber watches as they shoot him. She cries uncontrollably.

Analysis: In this dream, Amber's husband is a symbol of her own strength, which she feels she has lost because of her addiction.

The Math Class

Amber wakes up a second time, and then falls asleep again. The dream picks up where it had left off, with Amber crying over her husband's body. Suddenly she is back in the same parking lot, but this time she is in a math class that she hates. The math symbols look alien, and Amber does not care about the class: she just wonders if her husband is alive. At the same time, Amber feels strangely calm in the math class, as if she is safe from being attacked because she is at school.

Analysis: The math class is a metaphor about the school of life. Math is about rules, formulas, and standards that Amber needs, to turn her life around and measure up. The road back feels hard and unpleasant, like a math class. Yet Amber also feels safe in the math class. Something in her recognizes there is something valuable in the struggle to get back on track, a struggle that can lead to safety.

Death of Parents

The next night, Amber dreams that her parents have died, and she cries over her mother's body. She remembers how her mom smelled of fresh soap, then wakes up.

Analysis: The scene is a metaphor of pain over losing what is precious—the normal life and love Amber once had. Yet there is hope. Crying over her mother's body suggests that Amber longs for what she has lost, a deep longing that contains the seeds of healing and finding her way back. Each nightmare highlights vulnerability, loss of strength, and feeling trapped, as an emotional valley of pain that Amber lives through daily as she tries to overcome her disease of addiction. The final scene suggests that if she works at it, there is hope.

PRISON AS AN EXTREME LIFE CHALLENGE

A journey through the world of nightmares is not complete without a glance at the dreams of those behind bars. Whether guilty or innocent, contrary to glamorized movies, those who find themselves behind bars endure a living daily nightmare, as do their families.

A Spotlight on Dreams of Those Behind Bars

Richard Lovelace was a seventeenth-century British nobleman and poet who fought for equal rights and, for his trouble, was detained as a political prisoner. He wrote the famous lines "Stone walls do not a prison make, nor iron bars a cage." Lovelace died alone and penniless, yet his words live on as a testimony to a spirit that could not be broken. A lover of justice, Lovelace would be shocked that four hundred years later, jails in the United States hold four or five times more people than other countries, and sadly, they hold many who are innocent.

No one disputes the need for prisons, yet few dispute that justice is often undermined by outmoded laws and counterproductive procedures.

One issue that needs prison reform is nasty prison conditions. Another is the enormous tax burden that prisons impose on citizens. A third dirty secret is the toll in human suffering that an overly zealous prison system creates. The United States houses two million prisoners; add to that another ten to twelve million relatives and loved ones who suffer alongside, silently. For each imprisoned man or woman, the lives of countless unnamed children, spouses, family, and friends are also devastated and impacted. Prisons and unnecessarily harsh laws and procedures related to the incarcerated are a festering wound that politicians and communities must address. This is a sample of one prisoner's nightmares.

Prison Dreams—Harrison's Nightmares

Going to prison is bad enough when someone is guilty, and it's far worse for someone who is innocent, like Harrison. Through the details are irrelevant, Harrison's conviction highlights common miscarriages of justice that include a trial steamrolled by ambitious prosecutors, wins stacked with ambiguous and slanted evidence, and inept defense lawyers. Guilty or innocent—the focus here is on how a prisoner's shattered life shows up in dreams.

Sentenced to ten years for a crime he did not commit, Harrison arrived in prison and sank into the Dark Night of the Soul. Mentally, he beat himself up every day for believing he would be exonerated just because he was innocent. He kicked himself for allowing a lawyer to make decisions that he and his family did not like. He second-guessed everything a hundred times a day. So sad. So sorry. It was too late. Nightmares mirrored Harrison's turbulent suffering and that of his loved ones; once in a blue moon, a positive dream offered Harrison a tiny morsel of hope—a crumb just big enough to get him through another day.

Poker Dreams

Before he went to prison, Harrison enjoyed playing poker with buddies, when time allowed. Harrison knew his limits and never played beyond a small, predetermined budget.

After a rare positive prison dream, Harrison woke up elated, remembering a scene of holding a winning hand of four sevens.

Analysis: Mystics suggest that the number seven has a spiritual significance as God's blessing; Harrison did feel uplifted by the mystical hand of sevens.

In another poker dream, Harrison wins a hand with a pair of sevens and an ace kicker. In a third, while playing poker, Harrison shares his story with a fellow player, who says "Never give up."

The poker dreams transported Harrison to happier days, infusing a tinge of hope into his waking hours that felt like a living hell.

Laura Leaves Harrison

Prisoners often dream about their mate. Some dreams replay a hug or loving gesture; others are nightmares about bad things that happen to loved ones. Nightmares often highlight a common fear prisoners have—that a wife or girl-friend will walk away while they are in prison. Before his trial, Harrison's biggest fear was losing Laura, the woman he considered his true love. Other inmates fueled those fears by telling Harrison "They always walk way; sooner or later, they leave you."

In a nightmare that left Harrison shattered, he dreams Laura has left him for another man. In another nightmare, Laura stands in front of Harrison in a red dress, saying she has met and married someone else.

Harrison shook off the nightmares; they were only dreams. Nevertheless, the fears lingered. Though Harrison and Laura spoke daily by phone and she would visit often, Harrison's fear of losing Laura ravaged his emotions. And then, four years into Harrison's ten-year sentence, Laura did walk away with someone new.

A Visit from Dad

Harrison's psyche also provided a safe haven in his dreams. As compensation for his worn spirit,

> Harrison regularly dreamed that he was back home, far from the shouting, chaos, filth, and corruption that surrounded him in prison. In one dream, a song Harrison loves is playing; then the phone rings. It is a phone call from his dead father. Harrison had adored his dad; father and son were buddies. Harrison hears his dad's voice as plain as day, telling him that heaven is beautiful, and that he is with loved ones in the Great Beyond. Harrison shares his sorrows with his father. As his dad leaves, he says "Everything is going to be all right."

The dream visit uplifted Harrison beyond words; it felt so real. His beloved dad's parting words provided a deep well of strength for Harrison, for years.

Alice and the Squirrel

The Dreamer: Family and friends of those in prison suffer too. As a former colleague, Alice knew Harrison was a good man and believed in his innocence. She emailed words of comfort regularly, knowing that emails are an electronic lifeline for many behind bars. Feeling Harrison's anguish, one night Alice experienced a blood-curdling nightmare.

Alice looks into her backyard and sees a squirrel in a tree, jumping up and down. At first, it looks like the squirrel is playing. But as Alice looks closer, she notices that the squirrel is tied to a string, like a puppet, a string that is being yanked up and down, cruelly, against the creature's will. A large fishing hook, lodged inside the squirrel's mouth, holds the string, causing the creature great pain, as a nearby man swings the squirrel around in deliberate torture. As he does so, the man laughs, enjoying the helpless creature's pain. Though horrified, Alice can do nothing to help the captive animal. Finally the string breaks; terrified and exhausted, the squirrel escapes.

Analysis: Alice woke with a silent scream she could not utter, and her heart ached for days. She instinctively knew the nightmare echoed Harrison's suffering, a suffering no one could alleviate. Familiar with the facts of Harrison's case, Alice knew the nightmare portrayed the failure of the justice system, a failure that left Harrison dangling in prison, in excruciating pain. And though the implication was shocking, it did not surprise Alice that some, behind the scenes, took pleasure in Harrison's pain. She knew there had been monkey business in Harrison's case and hoped that one day, the truth would come to light. As Noel Coward once said, "It is discouraging how many people are shocked by honesty and disbelieve it, and how few respond in the same way, to deceit."

El sueño
de la razon

CHAPTER NINE

Common Nightmare Symbols

Dream dictionaries tend to mislead about the meaning of a dream symbol or character. A dream dictionary implies there is a single meaning for each symbol, like words in a regular dictionary. Not so. Dream characters and objects are like actors that take on roles that change with every story. Furthermore, the meaning of a person or object relates to the dreamer's unique, personal experience. A final note: It can be helpful to examine symbols as metaphors that bring up questions for the dreamer to answer, as in the following examples.

SYMBOLS AS METAPHORS

The most productive way to see what a symbol means is to examine how it fits into the overall story. Treat the character or object as if it is a mini story and see what questions the symbol brings up as a metaphor. To get a feel for what they mean, the symbols described in the following list are expanded into metaphors. The first few metaphors include examples of how to think a metaphor through. By turning a metaphor into a question, you ask yourself how the image may relate to a life situation, thoughts, or feelings. Once you see how that works, you can apply the question technique to any metaphor.

Note: These examples are "general what-ifs." For the true meaning of a dream symbol, always check your personal experience about the person or object, and weave your related memories back into the story.

Abuse
Whether the abuse that is portrayed is physical or emotional abuse, abuse speaks of a misuse of power or authority; it can also relate to someone who feels overwhelmed or mistreated.

Ask: Where do I feel overpowered or controlled? Who is being controlling? Is there someone around me who feels overwhelmed? Who holds power over me? Do I let others make too many decisions for me? Who is under my authority and how do I treat them? Have I misused my strengths?

Animals, Wild or Domestic
Animals in dreams often mirror human traits. They can also be plays on words and metaphors, associated with the animal. A pig can refer to a struggle with eating issues, or symbolize an intelligent, yet misunderstood, creature. As king of the jungle, a lion may hint of majestic qualities, or what feels dangerous. As a

vicious fighter, a hyena may reference a need to fight for oneself, or a bad temper. A wolf may point to issues of predatory instincts, or a seductive male.

Ask: Does someone I know have the qualities of the animal in my dream? Do I recognize its negative or positive traits in myself? How do I use those traits?

Attacks, Being Attacked

An attack is a display of anger or power; being attacked suggests a serious confrontation, or being overpowered.

Ask: Who expresses a lot of anger. Is bad temper an issue for me? How extreme are the portrayed angry feelings? Does someone or something make you angry lately? What skills do you have to cope with frustration? How well do you express what upsets you? When on the receiving end of anger, do you need to assert yourself more, or to communicate what bothers you?

Betrayed, Betrayal, Cheating

A dream of cheating on a mate or on an exam, or short-changing someone in a business deal, brings up issues of trust and betrayal.

Ask: Do you feel cheated in any way? Are there people you do not trust? Is there anyone you trust whose actions should be examined more closely? Are you cheating on your own ideals or standards by not living up to them, as you know you should?

Bugs and Insects

In the English language, a bug can be a play on words for "what bugs you" as a reference to what annoys or disturbs you. Bugs can be difficult to control and can cause injury and destruction. Ugly or dangerous bugs can point to a negative activity or attitude, or potential outcomes that could become ugly, dangerous, or disturbing.

Ask: What in my life bothers or annoys me? Do I have feelings or thoughts that are becoming difficult, or disturbing? Is there someone around me or a project or action, that is becoming negative or out of control? How well do I cope with what is annoying?

Cannibal, Cannibalism

Eating another's flesh violates a serious social norm. Ask questions about lines that are being crossed, either by you or by someone around you. Examine norms, morals, and standards that are important to you, and how you consider or apply them.

Chasing and Being Chased

You run from what scares you, so dreams of being chased highlight what makes you feel vulnerable and anxious. Unless you are confronted by real danger, running away is not normally a strategy for success, so images of being chased invite you to name your fears, face them, and find ways to handle what is scary.

Child in Danger

Caring for a child takes love and requires a long term commitment. Images of a child in danger put a spotlight on commitments that are not being honored or are not working out. It can also highlight how motivated someone may feel about their responsibilities. Ask whether a project needs help, or if a long-term goal needs attention. What happens to the child can parallel what is going on with an issue, and how things may turn out—unless you fix it.

Clowns: Scary or Evil Clowns and Faces

Normally, you see clowns at a circus or at a children's party. A happy clown evokes laughter and lighthearted feelings. A scary or evil clown suggests the opposite— what normally brings joy now creates pain and fear, highlighting emotions or situations that have turned sour. The scarier the clown, the more serious the fear or the issue.

Crashes, Collisions, Serious Accidents

Car or plane crashes are a common nightmare scene that bring to mind unexpected disasters, challenges, experiences that shock, or clashes in ideas or relationships. A crash can point to relationships heading toward a painful end, projects that can fall apart, or health symptoms which, if ignored, could surface as a surprise illness.

Death, Funerals, and Coffins

As the ultimate change and mystery that we encounter, images of death tend to relate to major life changes and to endings. How characters act and react to what is going on can be a hint about the change, or can highlight how the dreamer feels about changes, which can be impending or ongoing. The ending can hint how things will proceed or turn out.

Devil, Pact with the Devil

For many, seeing the devil in a dream invites the dreamer to confront what terrifies them. As a portrayal of evil, the devil can represent the dreamer's internal struggle with good and evil. Making a pact with the devil hints that the dreamer should examine whether they have hidden or opposing beliefs they are struggling with, and how those beliefs stack up in their life.

Disaster, Natural Disasters

A natural disaster can mirror a time of great challenge. A storm or flood can mirror a current challenge, or an obstacle heading your way. As a metaphor, a scene of disaster points to upheavals in career or relationships, health scares, and unexpected challenges that will feel overwhelming.

Dog Attacks, Dog Bites

As a generally friendly pet, dogs are normally seen as man's best friend. A dog that bites or attacks speaks of what is no longer friendly or caring. Nightmares about an attacking dog are common during a divorce or breakup, or as a mirror of someone who is ill-tempered. If a dog or animal attack feels extremely threatening and the dreamer is in a relationship with an abuser, the attack can signal actual danger.

Drowning

Water is often a symbol for feelings, and drowning speaks of emotions that are overwhelmed. Though most dreams about water relate to feelings, a few can be literal. If a dreamer has a water-related ailment or condition, such as water accumulating in the lungs, a dream about drowning can be a hint to see a doctor. Fishermen or boaters who dream of drowning might consider such images as a potential warning about bad weather or danger at sea.

End of the World, the Apocalypse

The end of world is a play on words for a major life change—as in the end of life as you now know it. Teenagers often dream about the apocalypse; when parents divorce or relocate, teens experience disruptions that can feel earth-shattering. Apocalyptic dreams can mirror feeling forced into change beyond one's control, or changes or feelings that feel scary and overwhelming.

Failure: Failing an Exam, Project, or Test

Failing is scary. Failure evokes shame and makes you feel vulnerable. Nightmares about failure invite you to examine your confidence and self-esteem. Or, failure in a dream can be a wake-up call about a neglected responsibility or task that needs your attention.

Falling

A scene of falling off a cliff or a building makes many wake up in a fright. Falling is a metaphor for losing control, losing emotional balance, or feeling disoriented and confused, as if you have no longer have solid ground to walk on. Falling can also be a play on words for "something that falls through" as a metaphor about a project or decision that is not working out well, as it currently stands. Examine what feels out of control, unsafe, or vulnerable, or what may be heading for a fall.

Ghosts

A ghost is a tie to the past. As a dream image, a ghost invites you to consider how issues from the past may be affecting you now. A friendly or helpful ghost can point to unused talents, activities, or attitudes from the past that you can dust off and constructively renew. Terrifying ghosts can point to past fears, traumas, and painful memories that still have an effect on you and therefore need healing.

Grim Reaper

While death as a dream image is about endings or major change, the Grim Reaper is the ringmaster who announces the change and ushers it in. As a negative image, dreams about the Grim Reaper tend to highlight a painful change or a serious, negative attitude that needs change. On rare occasions, as the symbol of death, the Grim Reaper can announce an actual, impending death.

Halloween, Halloween Costumes

Clothes are a calling card about how you feel; they mirror your attitudes and who you are. During Halloween, people put on scary costumes to have fun and collect goodies. Depending on the emotional context, nightmares with scary costumes can bring up negative or playful attitudes or emotions.

Jail, Prison, Being in Jail

You go to jail when you break the law. Being in jail suggests a need to review actions or thoughts that are out of bounds or heading in that direction. Images of police are a question about lawfulness, authority, and doing what is right. Jail or prison can also be a symbol of limitations and what makes you feel restricted or limited.

Monsters and Villains

Whether a dream scene depicts Frankenstein or a modern villain like Megatron from Transformer movies, dream monsters highlight fears, negative actions or thoughts, and emotions that may be overdone or getting out of control. Dreams are a lens through which you see the world. Constant scenes of monsters can hint that someone experiences life as scary or overwhelming—either in general, or due to a specific situation or person.

A Special Hint—Monsters in Children's Dreams

Dreams of monsters tend to mirror a child's fear, yet children typically cannot explain what scares them. It can be helpful to ask general questions about people or circumstances, and see if the child expresses something that does not feel good. If there are no clear answers, remind the child that he or she is strong enough to handle whatever comes their way. Tell them that if anyone or anything scares them, or does not feel right, even a little bit, that they should tell you about it. Such a reassurance leaves the door open for follow-up conversations, and can be all a child needs.

Murder, Killing, Getting Killed

Death and dying is about change or endings; killing is about aggression, as changes that feel forced on the dreamer. Getting killed in a violent way can suggest an unwanted change that someone wants to or needs to resist.

No Voice, Cannot Speak

Having no voice or being unable to speak is a metaphor about not feeling heard, or not being unable to communicate. Being unable to speak can raise questions about a dreamer's ability to assert themselves. Scenes may include images of being suffocated or unable to breathe.

Paralyzed, Trapped, Immobile

A nightmare about being paralyzed hints at feeling ineffective and helpless. Nightmares of being paralyzed or trapped can suggest a need to check your emotional pulse. Extreme anxiety, dread, or depression can leave a person feeling powerless and unable to act or react, as images of emotional paralysis. Paralysis can also be a metaphor about a less-important emotional issue like procrastination, as a hint about unfinished activities.

Rape, Gang Rape

Rape speaks to being overpowered and the misuse of power. It can point to issues that are forced on the dreamer, or to manipulation and misuse of authority. Scenes of rape raise questions about feeling emotionally violated or disrespected, emotionally or otherwise. Rape scenes can also raise questions about whether someone is being too passive, or is allowing themselves to be used by others to their own detriment.

Snakes, Reptiles

As a metaphor, snakes have a wide range of associations. A snake can mirror what undermines or threatens, or reference a sneak verbal attack like gossip, or being undermined in one's career. To those with a religious bent, a dangerous snake can point to temptations that the dreamer is grappling with, as a moral issue.

Stalked, Stalkers

Nightmares about being stalked or watched constantly can point to fears or anxieties about what others think, or can flag being overly concerned about what others think. Being stalked can also hint at a perfectionist streak, as a constant state of self-vigilance that disrupts the dreamer's peace of mind. If there is an actual menacing situation like domestic abuse in the dreamer's life, nightmares about stalking can be a heads-up that the dreamer needs to protect themselves. Take note: Statistics related to abuse sadly suggest that some possessive partners or exes with a history of being threatening become dangerous stalkers who do harm, even after the relationship ends.

Torture, Being Tortured

Torture is a scene of extreme pain or can register tension or emotions that are nearing a breaking point. If such images persist, it may help to consult a counselor.

Witches, Wizards

On the positive side, a witch or wizard can be a metaphor about opportunities and transformations that feel magical, like a new talent that unfolds and brings rapid success. A nightmare about a wicked witch or wizard can highlight something that feels evil and negative to the dreamer, whether real or imagined. A witch can reference actual acts of meanness or manipulation. Or, as a metaphor about someone nasty, a witch can register how you feel about someone, whether they are really that way or not, like the teen who had a nightmare that her mom was a wicked witch who put her on an ironing board and ironed her into a flat pancake. The story line said: Someone straightens another out. As the teen sought independence, she felt controlled and rebelled against rules and standards. As the teen's dream showed, mom stood her ground, hopefully with love. You go, mom!

Bonus Hint: Symbols as Metaphors

Whether the symbol or metaphor is scary or not, a symbol can be a play on words. Look for a variety of word plays in dream scenes such as common expressions, jingles, or song snatches that may contain a hidden meaning. For example, a dreamer saw a headless man walking by. The headless man was a play on words for "he lost his head" as a message that the dreamer was behaving in a rash manner. Someone else dreamed of a man whose torso was turned around. The top part of the man from the waist up faced backward, while his rear faced the front. The dreamer was familiar with the expression "doing something ass backward" as a comment about one of his activities.

ℱINAL THOUGHTS

The Author's Last Words on Nightmares

A miracle is a shift in perception
. . . from fear, to love.
—Marianne Williamson

No one ever explained nightmares to my satisfaction, a vacuum that gave me the incentive to ponder what nightmares mean and how they work. My original foray into dream analysis began with a blood-curdling nightmare about an old woman with an ax who stands behind a large wooden door at the top of an old staircase, ready to kill me. Though terrifying, I continue climbing, knock on the door, and as the old woman's ax strikes down at me, I wake up, screaming. As a nineteen-year-old, I had no idea what the dream meant; yet, strangely, I fell back to sleep feeling perfectly at peace. It took years before I understood this first "official" dream. Years later, I understood that the old woman mirrored hidden fears about examining myself through dreams. I did not know it then, but I passed the initiation into the unconscious and from that day forward, my psyche brought me wondrous messages through dreams about myself and my life.

A scary dream is a paradox. It is a bitter-tasting medicine for the mind and heart, yet the core of the nightmare holds a sweet center—a message that transforms! Nightmares are the dream type most often sent to my website—Interpretadream.com—for analysis. A terrified mother asks what a dream about the death of her child means; and, as covered in this book, it is extremely rare for a dream about death to mean that someone will actually die. Most times such dreams mirror a mom's personal fears.

If these meanderings about scary dreams enticed you to see nightmares in a new light—as friendly, helpful messages—Hurray! And if this book entices you to use the Five-Step Method to analyze dreams for your own happiness and welfare, I say: Hallelujah, my work is done. At least for now. . . .

I am grateful and amazed to share a lifetime of observations about nightmares with you!

INDEX

A

Abuse symbol, 184
Alice and the Squirrel nightmare, 182, 183
Alzheimer prevention, and sleep, 36
Amplification method of understanding
    symbols, 23
An Intruder Kills My Mom nightmare, 107,
    108
Animals symbol, 184, 185
Anniversary visits
    I Am So Sorry nightmare, 142, 143
    I Miss You So Much nightmare, 143
    Love Never Dies nightmare, 143, 144
Announcement of death nightmares
    Dead Dad in Search of Someone, 147,
    148
    Happy Trails to You, Until We Meet
    Again . . ., 148
Appearance Struggles nightmares, 58, 59, 60
Assassin's Death Threat nightmare, 46
Association method of understanding
    symbols, 22
Attack on Helpless Creatures nightmare, 75
Attacks symbol, 185
Awake you, 7

B

Bankrupt and Penniless nightmares, 170, 171
Betrayal symbol, 185
Betrayed nightmare, 70, 71
Black Wolf nightmare, 119
Break-In nightmare, 85, 86
Breaking the Law nightmare, 58
Bugs and insects symbol, 185

C

Cannibalism symbol, 186
Car Accident nightmare, 38–39
Carjacked nightmare, 133
Car Troubles nightmare, 85, 86
Cayce, Edgar, 70
Characters in nightmares, examining, 38
Chased nightmare, 175
Chasing symbol, 186
Cheating Husband nightmare, 100, 101
Chicken Crossing Road dream, 18
Child in danger symbol, 186
Claiming the Coveted Prize nightmare, 59
Clowns symbol, 187
Computer Hack nightmares, 89, 90–92, 93
Conversation with My Dead Father
    nightmare, 47, 48
Coping mechanism, 102
Crashes symbol, 187

D

Damn, Girl, You Look Good nightmare, 60
Dancing the Night Away nightmare, 134, 135
Dark Night of the Soul nightmares, 166,
    167–177
Dark side, embracing your, 42
Date Gone Wrong nightmare, 145
Dead, dream visits from
    anniversary, 142, 143–144
    comforting, 142, 143
    pets, 151, 152–153
    with a message, 144, 145–148
    near-death experiences, 137, 138
    prayers, 138, 139, 149

Dead Dad in Search of Someone nightmare, 149, 150
Dead Father Turns His Back on Me nightmare, 164, 165
Dead Mom Advises Teen nightmare, 144, 145
Death in dreams
    of beloved pets, 83, 84
    as grief about actual loss, 132, 133–136, 137
    by gunfire, 95, 96–97
    as a heads-up about a challenge, 125, 126
    as a literal warning, 80–83, 84
    as metaphor, 124, 187
    nightmares about, 126
    visits from deceased, 139, 140–153
Death of husband nightmare, 176
Deep Wound nightmare, 134
Defense mechanism, 104
Devil symbol, 187
Disaster symbol, 188
Dog attacks symbol, 188
Downward Spiral nightmare, 56
Dreams
    analyzing, 11–31
    long, story lines for, 20, 21
    messages, determining, 26, 27
    messages, five steps to a, 13–31
    messages, using, 14
    versus nightmares, 4
    warnings, 76–81
Drowning in a Sinking Ship nightmare, 115, 116, 117
Drowning symbol, 188
Drug addiction and nightmares, 176, 177, 178, 179
Dying Pigeon nightmare, 63, 64, 65

E

Emotions
    and dreams, 13
    and dreams, analyzing, 14, 15–17, 18
    nightmares that heal, 37, 38
    and trauma, 162
Empty Road nightmare, 85
End of the World symbol, 188
Eugene, Andy, 35
Extreme life challenges, and nightmares
    drug addition, 174–176, 177
    financial problems, 170, 171–173
    prison, 177, 178–181

F

Failing an exam symbol, 189
Falling symbol, 189
Fatal Car Crash nightmare, 130
Fear, and nightmares, 33, 34
Feelings about dreams
    digesting, 15, 16
    labeling, 37
Ferris Wheel dream, 19, 20
Football dream, 13, 14
Funerals symbol, 187

G

Gaming and death, 126
Gang rape symbol, 191
Gang-Raped and Stabbed nightmare, 111
Generations of Love nightmare, 142, 143
Gentle nightmare selfies
    An Assassin's Death Threat, 46
    Conversation with my Dead Father, 47, 48
    Husband Leaves, 51, 52
    I am the Grim Reaper, 46, 47
    I Watch as My Wife is Abused, 53, 54
    Selling My Soul to the Devil, 49, 50, 51

Gestalt, 23
Ghost Girl nightmare, 65, 66, 67
Ghosts symbol, 189
Good Intentions Gone Bad nightmare, 106, 107
Greenberg, Aaron, 131, 132
Grief, death as, 132, 133–136, 137
Grim reaper symbol, 189
Groping a Mannequin in the Dark nightmare, 67, 68–69

H
Halloween symbol, 190
Happy Trails to You, Until We Meet Again . . . nightmare, 150
Health Warning nightmare, 131, 132
Highway Madman nightmare, 61, 62, 63
Husband Leaves nightmare, 51, 52

I
I Am So Sorry nightmare, 140, 141
I Am the Grim Reaper nightmare, 46, 47
I Cheat Regularly nightmare, 86, 87
I Miss You So Much nightmare, 141
"Internalizing" a concept, 118
I Watch as My Wife is Abused nightmare, 53, 54
Immobility symbol, 191
Injured Creature nightmare, 90, 91

J
Jail symbol, 190
Jane Fonda Visits nightmare, 59, 60

K
Keep Me Informed nightmare, 82
Killing a Dog nightmare, 130, 131
Kramer, Milton, 131, 132

L
Laura Leaves Harrison nightmare, 179, 180
Literal dream warnings
    ambiguous, 95, 96–101
    asking for a new dream, 79, 80
    death, 80, 81–92, 93
    determining if literal, 93, 94, 95
    features of a, 78, 79
Long dreams, story lines for, 20, 21
Love Never Dies nightmare, 141, 142
Lovelace, Richard, 177

M
Major Tooth Cracks nightmare, 91, 92
Many Are Trying to Kill Me nightmare, 130, 131
Marriage as a metaphor, 80
Masiak, Jolanta, 35
Math Class nightmare, 176, 177
McKinley, John, 35
Memory
    function of, 9
    and symbols, 24
Metaphors
    death as, 124
    marriage as, 80
    as "stand in" for a second meaning, 25
    symbols as, 184–193
    versus true warnings, 5, 7
Monsters metaphor, 190, 191
Morality issues, and nightmare selfies
    An Attack on Helpless Creatures, 75
    Betrayed, 70, 71
    description of, 70
    To Be or Not to Be . . . Together, 74
Mother, I am Here nightmare, 150
Mother in Handcuffs nightmare, 29, 30

Mother's Blessing nightmare, 146
Motorcycle Disaster nightmare, 80, 81
My Boyfriend is Dead nightmare, 129
My House Is on Fire nightmare, 98, 99

N

Near-death experiences, 137, 138
Nightmares
    analyzing, 11–31
    and fears and anxieties, 33–39
    as literal warnings, 78–101
    main points about, 6
    quiz about, 2, 3
    recurring, 103–121
    selfies, 43, 44–75
    self-revealing, 44–53, 54
    super-intense, 153–177
    symbols, common, 183–193
    that heal emotions, 37, 38
    understanding, 3, 4–5, 7
    and your limitations and negative
        characteristics, 41
    warnings, literal or symbolic, 93–101
    welcoming, 1
No Place to Shower nightmare, 27, 28
No voice symbol, 191
Not Yet Recovered nightmare, 149

O

On Fire nightmare, 30, 31
On the Brink of a Huge Eruption nightmare,
    88, 89
Overpowering Invasion nightmare, 87, 88

P

Pact with the Devil symbol, 187
Painful ending, death as a, 129, 130–131,
    132
Paralyzed symbol, 191

Perls, Fritz, 23
Pet dreams, 153–155
Plane Crash Kills My Family nightmare, 108,
    109, 110
Playing Happily in Still Water nightmare, 152
Poker Dreams nightmare, 179
Police Office Dreams of Death by Gunfire
    nightmare, 95, 96–97
Positive change, death as a, 126, 127, 128
Post-Traumatic Stress Disorder and
    nightmares, 158, 159–162
Prayers
    uniting the living and the dead, 140, 141
    visit from dead person who needs, 151–152
Prison
    and nightmares, 179, 180–183
    symbol, 190
Projection, and nightmare selfies
    Downward Spiral, 56
    Dying Pigeon, 63, 64, 65
    Ellen's Appearance Struggles, 58, 59–60
    Ghost Girl, 65, 66, 67
    Groping a Mannequin in the Dark, 67,
        68–69
    Highway Madman, 61–63
    and psyche, 55
    reason for, 54, 55
    Self-Inflected Torture, 57
    teen's nightmare, 56, 57
Psyche
    and awareness of upcoming event, 123
    and dream messages, 26, 27, 167
    and dreams, nightmares, and the mind,
        7, 8–9
    and emotional rut, 15, 16
    and enthusiasm, 12
    and evaluation of nightmares, 77

Psyche *(continued)*
    and feelings, 14, 15
    how it works, 8, 9
    and mechanics of dream symbols, 25
    and projection, 44, 45, 54
    and self-revealing nightmares, 44

R
Rage beneath Still Waters nightmare, 166, 167
Rape symbol, 191
Reactions to dreams, digesting, 15, 16
Real or fake dreams, 71
Recurring nightmares
    coping and repression, 104
    hints about, 105
    linked to a recent event, 111, 112–114, 115
    that originate in a distant experience, 106,
        107–110
    teenager's, 117, 118–121
Rapid Eye Movement (REM), 35, 157
Reptiles symbol, 192

S
Scares, positive effects of, 5
Scary Stranger nightmare, 114, 115
Selfie nightmares
    Appearance Struggles, 58, 59, 60
    Assassin's Death Threat, 46, 47
    Attack on Helpless Creatures, 75
    Betrayed, 70, 71
    Conversation with My Dead Father, 47, 48
    Downward Spiral, 56
    Dying Pigeon, 63, 64, 65
    Ghost Girl, 65, 66, 67
    Groping a Mannequin in the Dark, 67,
        68–69
    Highway Madman, 61–63

    Husband Leaves, 51, 52
    I Am the Grim Reaper, 46, 47
    I Watch as My Wife is Abused, 53, 54
    Selling My Soul to the Devil, 49, 50, 51
    Teen's, 56, 57
    To Be or Not to Be . . . Together, 74
Self-revealing nightmares, 44–73
Selling My Soul to the Devil nightmare, 49,
    50, 51
Sensitive individual nightmares, 7, 165, 166–168
Shootings and Killings nightmares, 120–121
Sleep and Alzheimer's prevention, 36
Sleeping Prophet, 70
Sleepwalking, research about, 3
Snakes symbol, 192
Snoozing Among the Scrubs nightmare, 151
Something Special is Gone nightmare, 134, 135
Soul, 8
Spiritual Warning nightmare, 88, 89
Staircase to Heaven nightmare, 153
Stalked by My Abusive Ex nightmare, 112, 113
Stalked by My Dead Father nightmare, 163
Stalker symbol, 192
Story line
    analyzing, 18, 19–20, 21
    creating a, 13
    matching to an area of your life, 13, 21,
        22, 24
Stress
    dreaming as an antidote to, 36, 37–39
    and nightmares, 34, 35
Sudden Attack nightmare, 81, 82
Superconscious, 8
Super-intense nightmares
    and drug addiction, 174, 175–177
    of prisoners, 177, 178–181

and PTSD, 156, 157–160
and sensitive people, 165, 166–168
trauma and, 161, 162–164, 165
types of, 156
Symbols, dream
common, 179–189
determining what they mean, 22–23
function of, 26
mechanics of, 25
and personal memories, 24
putting on hold, 19, 21
relating it to your experience, 13, 14

T

Tables are Turned nightmare, 92, 93
Teenagers' nightmares
Chased by Dinosaur, 167
Loses Her Best Friend, 135, 136, 137
recurring, 114, 115–116, 117
Sees an Endangered Llama, 168
Self-Inflicted Torture, 57
Thieves Scale the Bedroom Walls nightmare, 90, 91
Thugs in My Driveway nightmare, 85
To Be or Not To Be . . . Together nightmare, 74
Tolle, Eckhart, 166
Torture symbol, 192
Trapped symbol, 191
Trauma
and emotions, 160
and nightmares in combat veterans with PTSD, 161–162
and nightmares in the general population, 7, 163, 164, 165
True warnings versus metaphors, 5, 6

U

Unconscious, 7

V

Victim of Financial Scam nightmares, 171, 172–173
Visit from Dad nightmare, 180, 181

W

War veterans
nightmares, 159, 160, 161
studies, 131, 132
Weddings and Dead Relatives nightmare, 82, 83
What Lies Beyond the Grave nightmare, 127, 128
Who Stole My Car? nightmare, 112, 114, 115
Wild animals metaphor, 184
Williamson, Marianne, 194
Witches symbol, 192, 193
Wizards symbol, 192, 193
Woman with an Ax nightmare, 196

Y

You Are Still My Little Girl nightmare, 143
You Have Two Months to Live nightmare, 127

Z

Zie, Lula, 35

ABOUT THE AUTHOR

STASE MICHAELS has an M.A. in Psychology from the College of William and Mary and a second M.A. in Transpersonal Studies from Atlantic University. Drawing on four years of research with combat veterans, Michaels wrote three theses on sleep and trauma, taught dreams as a college course, and presents seminars across the U.S. and Canada. As the author of several books on dreams, Michaels says, "I've used dreams since age nineteen and know that dreams brilliantly provide accurate answers, practical insights, and bring out the best in you."

Well-versed in modern mystical theory with a special eye to the work of Edgar Cayce, Michaels uses dreams and meditation as her main focus. She points to dreams and the unconscious as a new, yet uncharted, frontier—waiting to be harnessed as a potent source of problem-solving for medical researchers, scientists, and inventors.

As a citizen of both Canada and the United States, Michaels lived in Virginia for twenty-eight years; she now resides in Toronto, Canada.

Her website interpretadream.com gives free information on dreams including a library of dream interpretations.

IMAGE CREDITS